The Only Three Discipline Strategies You Will Ever Need

Essential Tools for Busy Parents

Chick Moorman and Thomas Haller

Personal Power Press
Merrill, MI

The Only Three Discipline Strategies You Will Ever Need

Essential Tools for Busy Parents

Library of Congress Catalogue Card Number: 2007931102

ISBN 978-0-9772321-4-7

Personal Power Press
P.O. Box 547, Merrill, MI 48637

Cover Design
Zachary Parker/kadak graphics
kadakgraphics@cableone.net

Book Design
Connie Thompson/Graphics etcetera: connie2@lighthouse.net

TABLE OF CONTENTS

INTRODUCTION

Parents often find themselves struggling with discipline issues. Children whine, cry, and talk back. They pout, tease, or bully. They obsess over video games, visit inappropriate sites on the Internet, or hit their brother.

Some children get poor grades. Others wipe peanut butter on their pants, pee in their beds, or forget to do their chores. Some stay out past curfew, track dirt into the house, spill milk, slam doors, or use inappropriate language.

The adults want a clean room and the child wants to play. Parents announce bedtime and the children stall and delay. Mom buys goldfish and her daughter forgets to clean the fishbowl as promised. After a frustrating search, Dad finds his new hammer left by one of his children rusting in the backyard.

In response to the many challenges that children present, parents employ a variety of discipline techniques.

Some parents give quiet explanations. Others use behavior management charts colorfully decorated with stars and stickers. Some offer rewards, praise, or eloquent lectures. Other strategies often used by parents to gain compliance include yelling, spanking, bribing, threatening, pouting, giving children the silent treatment, dispensing guilt, shaming, ordering, criticizing, and nagging. Some punish children into submission with an escalating series of consequences.

None of these strategies are effective. They all create tension, resistance, and distance. None are respectful or loving. They are all manipulative and controlling. They foster temporary obedience to an outside authority, not the development of an internal guidance system that can be used for personal direction. They train kids to mind, not to develop self-discipline, self-reliance, or self-motivation. These parenting strategies do children's thinking for them rather than teach children to think for themselves. They do not help children create a strong sense of personal power.

This book will ask you to eliminate the controlling, manipulative strategies listed above. They don't work and they won't help you become the parent you always wanted to be. It will ask you to consider learning and using three strategies that *do* work, strategies that help children grow into responsible, caring, confident young adults, strategies that allow you to treat the important and sacred role of parenting with the respectful attention it deserves.

Three discipline strategies are all you will ever need to become an effective parent. That's right, just three.

You may wonder how there can be only three discipline strategies and how three would be enough to raise responsible children. Consider color. Did you know there are only three primary colors? They are red, blue, and yellow. All other colors are variations of those three. Those three colors can be put together in different combinations that make all the colors of the rainbow.

Just as there are only three primary colors, there are only three primary discipline strategies. All other useful discipline strategies are variations of these three - *The One-Minute Behavior Modifier, The Dynamic Discipline Equation,* and *The Positive Anger Explosion* - all of which you will learn from reading this important book.

Think of it this way. If you were a carpenter and you had to walk miles to work and could only take three tools with you, which ones would you take? Our guess is you would take a hammer, a screwdriver, and a saw. Those are the three you would need most, the three you would most likely use, the three that would give you the best chance of completing most jobs. The same holds true of the only three discipline strategies you will ever need. They are the ones you need most, the ones you will most likely use, and the ones that will give you the best chance of completing most parenting jobs.

The three strategies we present in this book can be taken with you everywhere you go. They make for light travel. You don't have to learn thirty-five parenting techniques, become skilled at each, and lug them with you on vacation as you visit relatives or the amusement park. You only need three.

- Are you stressed? Running out of time? You only need three discipline strategies.

- Are you dealing with young children, teens, or adolescents? It doesn't matter. You only need three.

- Do you live on a farm in Iowa, downtown in New York City, or in a resort hotel in Cancun, Mexico? You only need three.

- Are you a single parent, see your kids on the weekends, or have a spouse who supports and encourages your parenting style? No matter. You only need three. Are you getting the picture? These discipline strategies are universal.

Having only three strategies to learn makes your parenting life easier. You don't have to become skilled at twenty different techniques. It is easier to master three than to work at developing a skill set of fifteen. You only have three to remember, three to practice, and three to use with tots or teens.

Worrying about what to do when your kid whines will be a thing of the past. Trying to figure out what to do when your teen talks back to his grandfather will no longer be difficult. Coming up with a plan for dealing with your daughter's homework procrastination will not be a struggle. This book will provide the answers, as well as give you the skills and confidence to put the strategies into practice.

Chapter One, *"The One-Minute Behavior Modifier,"* will help you learn a technique for eliminating negative behaviors. Whining, back talk, pouting, teasing, bragging, disowning responsibility for actions, and other inappropriate behaviors can be greatly reduced or eliminated in your family by using this one-minute strategy. You will learn how to help your children by making the undesired behavior conscious and giving real reasons why it's inappropriate. In addition, you will learn to teach desirable replacement behaviors so your children will have a way to get their needs met without exhibiting the undesired behavior.

In **Chapter Two,** *"The Dynamic Discipline Equation,"* you will learn how to hold your children accountable for their actions and behaviors with love and consistency. By incorporating this equation into your family discipline plan you will help your children see the cause and effect relationship between their behaviors and the outcomes which follow. You will reduce your stress when holding children accountable and discover a meaningful way to determine appropriate consequences. You will also learn the three special words you can use to help your children make a conscious connection between cause (their choices and behaviors) and effect (the outcomes which follow).

Chapter Three, *"The Positive Anger Explosion,"* describes techniques that will allow you to communicate annoyance, irritation, and frustration in a way that lets your child know that you are clearly angry, yet refrains from attacking character or wounding the spirit. When you are in the midst of separating emotions it will help you to communicate in a way that is honest, direct, and encourages appropriate action on the part of your child.

Chapter Four, *"Putting It All Together,"* will show you how the only three discipline strategies you will ever need are connected and interrelated. You will see how there is no order of use for the three strategies and that any one of the three could be used first. You will understand how these strategies can be strung together in various combinations to produce the positive results you want with your children.

All the names in this book are fictitious, although the events and examples are real, drawn from incidents we have seen, personally experienced, or been told about at workshops or during parent coaching or therapy sessions. They are real stories from real people who work with real children. On occasion, we have combined more than one incident into one concise example.

It is no accident that you hold this book in your hands. Your wanting it has helped bring it into existence. Thank you for attracting it into your life and into the lives of your children. They are worth it, and so are you. Best wishes for becoming the parent you always wanted to be.

Chick Moorman and Thomas Haller

Chapter One

THE ONE-MINUTE BEHAVIOR MODIFIER

Are you tired of listening to whining, put-downs, excuse giving, back talk, exaggeration, interrupting, teasing, gossip, or other unproductive behaviors on the part of your children? Have you had your fill of watching them talk with their mouth full; use their hands instead of silverware to eat; hit or kick siblings; waste material; or leave their belongings scattered around the house?

If so, the One-Minute Behavior Modifier is for you. This quick and highly effective discipline strategy is a verbal skill designed to modify and eliminate negative behaviors in your children by helping them learn to replace those behaviors with more desirable ones.

Chauncy, age five, and Letrell, age four, sat on the picnic table sharing a Coke. Nearby, their grandfather tended to the bonfire he had burning in the fire pit.

Unintentionally, Chauncy took a few more turns with the Coke than did his younger cousin Letrell. And when the can was nearly empty, Chauncy chugged the remaining liquid.

When Letrell picked up the can to take his next turn and realized the soda was gone, he quickly launched into a behavior he had used many times before, one that had been extremely effective for him in the past. He assumed the victim stance and began to whine.

"Chauncy drank up all the Coke," he complained to his grandfather in a whiney tone. "He had more turns than I did. It's not fair."

The boys' grandfather never hesitated. "Letrell," he replied, "That is whining. Whining doesn't work with me. It does-

n't work with me because I have trouble hearing and under-standing what you want when you whine. What works with me is to talk in a normal voice, using a normal tone and normal volume. If you do that, sometimes you get what you want. Sometimes you don't, but it's your only hope."

Having never been talked to that way before, Letrell's eyes got big and he stared briefly at his grandfather before he changed his tone and stated in a normal voice, "Chauncy got more turns than I did and I didn't get very much."

Letrell's grandfather replied, "Thank you for choosing a normal voice. That makes what you want clear to me. Sounds like you're still thirsty."

"I am," said his young grandson. "Then let's look at some options for how to solve that problem," his grandfather suggested.

After brainstorming several possibilities, Letrell decided to go to the house and get another Coke.

This grandfather used verbal skills that were effective and time efficient. His grandson stopped whining. Both boys learned that whining doesn't work with their grandfather and that sometimes you can solve your own problem. This successful conclusion was orchestrated by an adult who was aware of the One-Minute Behavior Modifier, as well as how to apply it with the important children in his life.

This first discipline strategy asks you to take the teaching stance. It calls on you to identify the unwant-ed behavior, help your child become conscious of it, and then teach an appropriate replacement behavior to supplant the old one. That's what Letrell and Chauncy's grandfather did.

This is not a get-after-them-after-the-fact technique. It's an intermediary and important step that occurs immediately when you notice the undesired behavior and before you move to implementing consequences. It's an effort to be proactive and prevent the need for holding the child accountable, which is an important discipline step that we will strongly advocate in a later chapter.

The One-Minute Behavior Modifier has two stages: *Planning* and *Implementation.*

Planning

Before you can successfully implement the One-Minute Behavior Modifier some strategic planning is in order. This is best done in a five-step process.

Step One

Choose a behavior. Pick one that you are frustrated with, one you would like to have eliminated in your home. It could be whining, the behavior Letrell attempted to use with his grandfather. It could be taunting, crying, belittling, or any other behavior that you want to end.

Step Two

Give the behavior a name. If you can name it, you can tame it. A short, descriptive name that you will use every time you refer to this behavior will work best.

It is critical that you invest time making sure the name you choose is a specific behavior and not an inference. Names like "rude" or "disrespectful" are too general. Those terms mean different things to different people.

"Rude," "disrespectful," "mean," "selfish," "conceited," and "crybaby" are judgments, inferences that you make based on a behavior you have seen or heard. They do not identify the behavior accurately. Inferences do not bring the behavior to the child's conscious awareness in a way that he can process effectively. The more specific you can get in naming the behavior, the more accurate the picture you create in the child's mind of the behavior that needs to be eliminated. The goal here is to give the child one strong picture in their mind of the behavior, a clear picture of what the behavior actually is.

Examples:

Inference	**Behavior**
(abstract, general)	*(specific, descriptive)*
Rude	Using put-downs
Mean	Hitting
Selfish	Grabbing handfuls of cookies
Conceited	Exaggerating
Crybaby	Crying
Disrespectful	Interrupting
Disgusting	Talking with your mouth full
Discourteous	Forgetting to be appreciative
Shy	Ignoring a question

You can name the behavior "whining" or "verbal manipulation." You can call it "cussing" or "inappropriate language." As long as the name you choose for the behavior is descriptive, what you call it is less important than sticking firmly to the name you did select. Children get confused if you call their behavior "teasing" the first time, "taunting" the second time, and "bullying" another time. Whatever name you choose for this behavior, keep that same name until you are satisfied the behavior has been eliminated.

Step Three

Determine a reason why the behavior you want to eliminate is inappropriate. This could be because teasing often results in the other person feeling hurt, cussing sounds dirty and tells the world your communication skills are lacking, or interrupting denies the speaker an opportunity to finish his thought.

Use of the word *because* is important here. *Because* is a word of influence. People are more likely to go along with a suggestion when you attach a *because* to it. When you give children a reason, they are less likely to resist *because* they see the purpose for the behavior you desire.

Step Four

Determine a behavior that is appropriate to replace the undesirable one. Whining could be replaced with talking in a normal voice, normal tone, and normal volume. Using your words to tell me what you want is preferred to crying. While name-calling in the family is inappropriate, telling your sister exactly why you are mad at her is not.

"I don't care about the new behavior," a father told us recently at one of our parent training seminars. "I just want my son to stop the old one."

Simply stopping the inappropriate behavior is not enough. You can stop your child from doing a behavior. You can stop her fifteen times in a row if you choose. But if you don't teach her a new and acceptable behavior to replace the old behavior and have her practice it, she will go right back to the familiar one. This is a critical step in using the **One-Minute Behavior Modifier.** You need to have a new behavior to replace the old, undesirable one or you will not get the results you desire.

Step Five

Prepare a verbal statement to use when the undesirable behavior occurs. When you have designed a statement to your liking, practice it and commit it to memory so you can immediately deliver it any time you see or hear the behavior you are working on eliminating.

There are three important components that should go into your verbal statement.

1. Identify the behavior.

Name the child and name the behavior.

> *"Chauncy, that's whining."*
> *"Roberto, that is a put-down."*
> *"Lawrence, that's disowning responsibility for your
>   actions."*
> *"Tamiko, that's what we call taunting."*

Notice that this piece of the verbal statement does not

ask the child to stop the behavior. This is not a tell-them-what-to-do piece. It is an *identification* piece. You are simply identifying the behavior by calling it by name and bringing it to the child's attention.

Your children do not always know what taunting, whining, or disowning responsibility actually are. This piece helps them get clear in their minds what behaviors are considered whining and which ones are not. Remember to make the behavior specific and eliminate inferences.

For the second part of the identification stage, use one of the following two options. Do not do both. Some behaviors you are attempting to eliminate will sound better using the first option. Others will sound better with the second.

One option is to say, *"We don't do that in this family."*

Other versions of this same piece are:

> *"That works against our family beliefs."*
> *"That is in opposition to the norms we live by here in this home."*
> *"That's not how we treat each other here."*
> *"That doesn't sound as respectful as we like to be in this family."*

So far, the One-Minute Behavior Modifier verbal statement would sound like this . . .

> *"Roberto, that's a put-down. We don't do that in this family."*
> *"Tamiko, that's what we call taunting. That is not how we treat each other here."*

A second option you can use after naming the child and naming the behavior is to say, "That doesn't work with me." This option fits well with whining, disowning responsibility for actions, making excuses, and similar behaviors.

> *"Chauncy, that's whining. Whining doesn't work with me."*
>
> *"Latice, that's excuse giving. I don't accept excuses."*
>
> *"R. J., that's back talk. When you choose that behavior, it not only doesn't work with me, you usually end up in more trouble than you were to begin with."*

2. State a reason.

Add a *because* to your verbal statement immediately following the identification piece.

> *"Chauncy, that's whining. Whining doesn't work with me* because I have trouble hearing what you're saying. It's not an effective way to get what you want."
>
> *"Roberto, that's a put-down. We don't do that in this family* because it creates divisiveness and generates angry feelings."
>
> *"Tamiko, that's what we call taunting. Taunting violates the family norms we live by* because respect and honest communication are missing."
>
> *"Latice, that is excuse giving. I don't accept excuses* because if I do I'll encourage you to get good at coming up with excuses rather than completing your responsibilities."

"R. J., that's back talk. When you choose that behavior, it not only doesn't work with me, it also means you'll end up in more trouble than you were to begin with because that style of language is not respectful or solution oriented."

3. Teach a new behavior.

The next step with The One-Minute Behavior Modifier is the most important. It is to teach the new behavior. This is the replacement behavior that you want the child to use instead of the behavior he has been choosing up to this point.

"Chauncy, that's whining. Whining doesn't work with me. It's not an effective way to get what you want because I have trouble hearing what you're saying. What works with me is to talk in a normal voice, using a normal tone and normal volume. When you do that, sometimes you get what you want. Sometimes you don't, but it's your only hope."

"Roberto, that's a put-down. We don't use put-downs in this family because it creates divisiveness and generates angry feelings. What we do here is tell the other person how we are feeling and what we would like to have happen."

"Tamiko, that's what we call taunting. Taunting violates the family norms we live by because respect and honest communication are missing. When we're angry with another family member, we share how we are feeling and we tell the other person why."

"Latice, that is excuse giving. I don't accept excuses because if I do I'll encourage you to get good at coming up with excuses rather than completing your responsibilities. The procedure that we use in this family is to plan ahead, prioritize, and accept responsibility for the choices we make."

"R. J., that's back talk. When you choose that behavior it not only doesn't work with me, it also means you'll end up in more trouble than you were to begin with because that style of language is not respectful or solution-oriented. If you want to communicate your frustration to me, say, 'I'm frustrated,' and tell me why."

Here are more examples of verbal statements incorporating all three components of the One-Minute Behavior Modifier.

"Danielle, that is telling the wrong person. Telling me won't help you get a turn because the person that needs to hear that you want a turn is your sister. What works best here is to tell Maribeth, 'I would like a turn with the purple crayon soon.'"

"Mickey, we call that disowning responsibility for your actions. In this family we don't disown by blaming others because the only person we can ever control is ourselves. So what we do here is take responsibility for the part we played in the situation and accept the consequences. In this case it would sound like this . . ."

"Melissa and Brenda, that's excessive noise during study time. Excessive noise is not appropriate here because it distracts others and deprives us all of hav-

ing a quiet time to concentrate. What is appropriate during this important time is to respect the study time of others by whispering if you feel a need to share something with each other."

"Sondra, that is space invading. Space invading is not appropriate because it crowds your sister and prevents her from enjoying the story. What is helpful here is to find a spot on the couch where you have the room you need and allow others to have their own space."

"That is exaggerating, Devi. Exaggerating is inappropriate in our home because it creates a distorted view of the situation. What works well with us is to give an accurate account of the incident."

"Jeremy, that is looking to someone else to solve your problem. Looking to others to bail you out of a predicament is not effective because you don't learn how to handle the situations you create or how to be responsible for your choices. As a teenager in this family, looking inside yourself for solutions is what is important. What have you thought of so far?"

"Stan, that's pouting. Pouting doesn't work with me because I can't read minds and I don't know what you want. Your best hope for getting what you want is to tell me in words. When I understand your concerns, we can see if we can work it out."

"Chipper, that is interrupting. In this family we don't interrupt when Mommy is on the phone because it distracts people on both ends of the conversation. What you can do if you want my attention when I'm on the phone is put your hand on my

hand. I'll squeeze it to let you know that I know you want a turn, and I'll give you attention when I find a break in the conversation."

"Natalie, that's what we call gossip. Gossip is not a helpful behavior because the other person is not here and has no way of rebutting your remarks. The person you're talking about can be harmed by untrue rumors. Please wait until Charley is present and ask him directly about what you heard."

Using a planning form

When you're first learning the skill of preparing a **One-Minute Behavior Modifier** and sending your verbal statement, it's often helpful to use a planning form such as the one below.

Behavior:

_____
_____
_____

Name the child, name the behavior:

_____
_____
_____

Add option one or option two:

One: "We don't do that in this family."
Two: "It doesn't work with me."

Include a because or reason:

_____

_____

_____

State the new behavior:

_____

_____

_____

Example:

Five-year-old Justin had developed the habit of ignoring requests from his mother when she wanted to tell him something. This behavior was reoccurring and happened so frequently that his mother decided to take action using the One-Minute Behavior Modifier. That night she created the following plan using the preceding form.

Behavior: Ignoring a request

Name the child, name the behavior: Justin, that is ignoring a request when I ask you to do something.

Add option one or option two: We don't do that in this family.

Include a because or reason: Because I can't tell if you heard or understand the directions.

State the new behavior: What is helpful here is for you to respond the first time I ask by doing what I ask or telling me you heard.

The next time Justin ignored his mother's request she was ready. Since she had her verbal statement memorized, it rolled smoothly off her tongue like it was a natural response to his behavior. "Justin, that is ignoring a request when I ask you to do something. We don't do that in this family because I can't tell if you heard or understand the directions. What is helpful here is for you to respond the first time I ask by doing what I ask or telling me you heard."

Justin looked stunned for a moment and then replied, "I hear you and I'll do it after I finish reading this paragraph."

"Thanks," the pleased mother responded. "I appreciate knowing that you heard."

After you have picked the behavior to be modified and created your One-Minute Behavior Modifier statement, memorize it. When the behavior occurs - and it will - you'll be ready. You won't have to worry about fumbling around trying to find it or remember the carefully crafted response you created in your mind the night before.

Implementation

Once the planning stage has been completed, it's time to begin implementing that plan. Successful implementation has three major components.

1. Become a first-time responder.

Deliver your statement every time you hear or see the behavior. Make no exceptions. Become a first-time responder. First-time responders react the first time they hear or see the behavior. They do not ignore the undesired behavior once or twice hoping it will go away. It won't. Know this: *The behavior will not change until you change your approach to the behavior.*

The first time you hear teasing, use your verbal statement. Say, "Pablo, that's teasing. Teasing violates our family norm of respecting one another. We don't do that in this family because other people don't feel safe in a home where teasing is allowed. What we do here is take everyone's ideas seriously even if we don't agree with them. If you don't agree, say so and explain your views"

If you use your verbal statement sporadically, your children will quickly figure out that you do not respond consistently. It will then take much longer to extinguish the unwanted behavior. Your lack of consistent follow-through teaches your children that you are not serious enough about the behavior to stick with it. *With any discipline strategy, the kiss of death is inconsistency.* Be consistent.

Do not wait for a convenient time to use the One-Minute Behavior Modifier. Use it in church. Use it at the dinner table. Use it in the presence of relatives. Use it even if you have to walk into the other room or follow your child upstairs. Use it if you need to go outside to confront the behavior. Use it whenever and wherever you see or hear the undesired behavior.

You will be tempted to bypass your planning efforts from time to time. It's less effort to sit in your easy chair hoping the teasing you hear in the other room will diminish than it is to get up and move in that direction. Hollering, "Stop whining," takes less initial effort than using your prepared statement.

Remember, if this kind of haphazard and inconsistent response worked, you wouldn't be reading this book. You wouldn't have prepared your verbal statement using the planning form. You would have eliminated the behavior a long time ago. If your child's undesirable behavior persists it is time to change your behavior. Discipline yourself first, and that means disciplining yourself to become a first-time responder.

2. Repeat, repeat, repeat.

Children do not always learn the new behavior with one repetition of the One-Minute Behavior Modifier. It may take several repetitions over a period of days before they become conscious of what the behavior is, realize that is doesn't get them what they want, and that another behavior actually works for them on occasion.

It's quite possible that your child will need you to repeat the verbal statement several times in one day. If he whines at the breakfast table, implement the strategy. He may see the value of choosing a different behavior when attempting to get the cereal he likes but not transfer that learning to a different situation that develops in the car on the way to school. If he whines in the car, implement the strategy again. When, later in the day, you tell him that the cookies are for after dinner and he whines, you know the drill. Implement the strategy by sending your verbal One-Minute Behavior Modifier.

Your child is not a slow learner or a bad person if he

doesn't respond immediately by eliminating the ineffective behavior. Remember, it took him a long time to hone the skill of disowning responsibility. It could take several incidents of having the behavior brought to his attention for him to understand what you're talking about, become conscious of when he's using it, understand why it's undesirable, and experiment with the suggested replacement behavior to see if it works for him.

3. Act as if each time is the first time.

Speak to your child as if each incident is new or different. Treat each one as if it was a first-time occurrence regardless of how many times you have used this particular One-Minute Behavior Modifier.

Refrain from participating in the exercise of mental scorekeeping. Mental scorekeeping occurs when you keep track in your head and mention the number of times a behavior has occurred. Examples include:

> *"This is the third time today that I've reminded you about teasing your sister."*

> *"That's four. Four times you've whined, and you know it doesn't work with me."*

> *"That makes three times this week that I've had to tell you about exaggerating."*

> *"How many more times am I going to have to tell you that yelling is not appropriate in this family?"*

When you keep track of the number of times a behavior has occurred and mention it to your child, you take archeological baggage from the past and pull it into the present. This then increases the chance that the behavior will occur in the future because the child begins to see herself as being that way.

There is only one moment of power for you and for the child. That moment is now. The past is over. There is no way she can go back and not whine yesterday. That time is gone. She can only choose not to whine in this present moment. Concentrate on this moment and teach the alternative to whining as if you had never taught it previously.

The intention here is to confront a single occurrence of the behavior as it happens, not the pattern of behavior that has been spread out over several months or years. If you engage in mental scorekeeping, the weight of accumulated incidents will create added emotional and mental strain and prevent you from dealing with this present moment cleanly.

Situation I

Three-year-old Gabriella would occasionally hit the dog with her hand to signal him to move out of her way. Her parents thought it was funny and even laughed aloud a few times when it happened. They stopped laughing the day she hit a playmate because the neighbor was directly in her path.

That evening Gabriella's parents decided to use the One-Minute Behavior Modifier to teach her a more acceptable alternative to hitting. After designing a verbal statement together, they practiced saying it aloud until they could say it without looking at their notes. When they went to bed that night, Gabriella's mother and father felt confident and ready.

They didn't have to wait long to put their plan into practice. The next morning, Barkley, the family dog, was sitting in Gabriella's favorite chair when she came downstairs. The youngster went straight to the dog and hit him in the head with her hand. Both parents saw the incident. Gabby's mother spoke first.

"Gabriella, that is hitting. We don't hit animals or people in this family because it hurts them. What we do is call to Barkley, wait until he gets out of the chair, and then pet him for following directions." She then demonstrated the behavior that was preferred by calling to Barkley in a friendly voice. "Now, let me see you do it," she said to her daughter.

This determined mother put the dog back on the chair and gave her daughter an opportunity to practice the desired behavior. Afterwards, both parents gave Gabriella and the dog positive feedback for her efforts.

In this instance, Gabriella's parents added a new component. They had her actually practice the behavior. Hearing about the new behavior is important. Seeing it demonstrated by someone else is also valuable. Doing it yourself, with supervision, is another valuable step. Hearing it, seeing it, and doing it is a powerful combination that can be used to help your child learn valuable new skills as he or she moves through the ages and stages of childhood.

Situation II

Herman saw a toy on the top shelf of the store he was visiting with his mother. "I want a toy," he told his mother, pointing in the direction of a big metal truck. When she appeared to ignore his request and sped on down the aisle, Herman chose a new behavior, one designed to get his mom's attention and the toy he wanted. From his position in the front seat of the shopping cart, Herman began to scream and kick. He threw a tantrum.

"Herman, that's a tantrum," his mother informed him immediately. "A tantrum won't get you a toy because I don't respond to tantrums. If you want something you have to tell me with words and we can take it down and look at it and see how much it costs. Then we can see if you have enough money to get it. Say, 'I want to see that toy,' and see how that works."

Herman's mother correctly used the One-Minute Behavior Modifier when she became conscious of her son's tantrum behavior, but had this busy parent been alert earlier, she would have had no need to use it. Herman did use his words to ask for a toy. He said, "I want a toy." He actually used the precise behavior his mother desired.

Had she heard his request, this mother could have used that moment to reinforce the positive behavior by stating, "Thank you for using your words. Show me which one. Let's look at it and check the price."

Children often resort to using inappropriate behaviors when appropriate ones go unnoticed, are ignored, or don't get the results they had hoped for. Watch and listen for your children's efforts to use behaviors that are valued in your family. Help them see that these choices get them what they want some of the time. You might say something like, "Just because you use your words instead of whining doesn't mean you'll get more ice cream, but it ups your odds. When you tell me why you're angry without using cuss words, it doesn't mean I will immediately give you what you want. It does mean that we will have a mutually respectful discussion, the result of which is yet undetermined."

Situation III

Roberto and Arianna are adolescents, one year apart in age. Roberto is the oldest and also the biggest. He stands six inches taller and weighs forty pounds more than his sister. He uses his height, weight, and age difference to his advantage whenever he wants to exercise power at the expense of his younger sibling.

When Roberto wants his own way, he stands up, towers over his sister, waves his finger in front of her face, and occasionally pokes her. His parents have sent him to his room, yelled at him, ridiculed him, and put their fingers in his face. Not surprisingly, none of those maneuvers worked to eliminate the behavior on a long-term basis.

After attending one of our parent trainings, these parents switched tactics. They decided to use the One-Minute Behavior Modifier.

"Roberto, that's intimidation," his father told him when he next saw the behavior. "It's not appropriate in our family because it creates fear in the person being intimidated. Fear is not a motivator in our home. What we do here is use our most skillful words to try to convince the other person to do things our way. If that doesn't work, we accept their decision, sometimes reluctantly."

Roberto's parents had to use their verbal statement on several occasions before he figured out they were serious about creating a family environment free of fear-based tactics. Over time, he learned to speak up for himself skillfully while at the same time showing respect for the opinion of his sister.

The One-Minute Behavior Modifier is a useful way to communicate your family values and make them come alive in your home. Respect, responsibility, cooperation, charity, forgiveness, kindness, caring, love, integrity, and other important values can be incorporated into your home environment by teaching your children which specific behaviors demonstrate those character traits and which do not.

In the case above, fear-based manipulation was clearly not valued by Roberto's father. He used his son's attempts to intimidate his sister as a teaching opportunity to help Roberto realize he was living in an environment free of fear and was expected to demonstrate that value as well.

Situation IV

Tadihito Manura's stepdaughter, Carmen, began a new behavior shortly after her thirteenth birthday. The first time it occurred Tadihito was caught off guard. He wasn't even sure what had happened. He just knew he felt uneasy and that something inappropriate had just taken place.

The second time she used the behavior Tadihito knew he would be employing the One-Minute Behavior Modifier with it eventually. But he still wasn't quite sure what the behavior was. He didn't have a name for it. "I felt manipu-

lated" he told us at a recent parent training where we were helping him learn to train other parents in the Parent Talk System. "I can tell you I felt slimed, " he told the participants at the seminar. "It felt icky, like I needed to wipe myself off."

Tadihito was thinking about naming the behavior "manipulation" because he was sure her actions were a form of manipulation, but that name still didn't seem quite accurate. Before he made a firm decision, his stepdaughter manifested the behavior again. "I knew immediately what it was, then," he said. "It's as if I needed three repetitions before I could understand it. That third time it came through loud and clear. Carmen came up to me at a middle-school basketball game and she launched into a sexually charged manipulative maneuver. She turned into a cross between a pop star diva and an entitled princess right before my eyes. She smiled, winked, put her hands together, and swayed back and forth. In a real high-pitched voice she asked, "Tad, will you give me a dollar for a Pepsi? You like me, don't you? It's just a dollar. Wouldn't you do that for me? I know you like me. Come on, please?" I almost barfed right on the spot," he went on. "The behavior was so disgustingly inappropriate. It was flirty and sexual and not how we want our children getting their needs met."

"I was in the middle of your training at the time and had practiced using the One-Minute Behavior Modifier with other behaviors in our family. So I didn't even have to write out a statement. I just looked her right in the eye and said, without thinking about it, "Carmen, that's sexual and flirty. It's not appropriate in our family because it is not a healthy way to get what you want. In addition, it doesn't work with me because I am not manipulated by sexual gyrations. What works with me in a case like this is if you use a normal voice and say, "Tad, I'm thirsty and I don't have a *dollar for a Pepsi. Will you treat me?""*

Tadihito reported that his stepdaughter immediately stood up straight. She stopped wiggling, smiling, and sending sexual signals. She switched back to her normal thirteen-year-old voice and tone and said, "Tad, I'm thirsty and I don't have a dollar for a Pepsi. Will you treat me?" He gave her a dollar and off she went to rejoin her friends.

The good news, according to Tadihito, is, "I never saw that behavior again."

It's not surprising that Tadihito never saw that behavior again. Children use behaviors because they work for them. Kids whine because whining works. One child fights because fighting works for him. Another runs away from fights because running away is the behavior that works for him. Pouters pout for only one reason. Pouting works for them. *If the behavior stops working, children stop working the behavior.* Are you ready to demonstrate to your child that his inappropriate behavior is no longer going to work?

Situation V

Eleven-year-old Armand developed the habit of placing the responsibility for the questions he wanted answers to on someone else. He would typically say to his parents:

"Kristy wants to know if I can go upstairs and play Monopoly in her room."
"Jackson wants to know if I can spend the night at his house this Friday."
"My friends want to know if I can go ice skating with

them this weekend."

Kristy, Jackson, and Armand's friends may want to know, but Armand has the stronger need to know. And he is not accepting full responsibility for his inquiries.

Recently, when Armand asked, "Jackson wants to know if I can spend the night at his house this Friday," his father was ready. He replied, "Armand, that is disowning responsibility for your question. When you ask as if someone else wants to know, the answer is always NO. That's because I only consider requests that are delivered by the person who really wants to know. So if it's Jackson who wants to know, the answer is NO. If you want me to consider the question seriously, you need to begin your question with an "I" statement. Say, "I want to know if I can stay overnight at Jackson's this Friday."

Armand never hesitated. He immediately demonstrated understanding of the situation and responded accordingly. "I want to know if I can stay overnight at Jackson's this Friday," he said.

"Well, let's explore that possibility," his father answered, reinforcing his son's effort to ask in a manner that took ownership for his question.

Armand's father demonstrated with his words that he understood an important principle contained in the One-Minute Behavior Modifier technique. The technique is designed to teach, and in order for Armand to learn, it is necessary for his father to use his words to paint a clear picture of the undesired behavior as well as one of the preferred behavior.

"Armand, that is disowning responsibility for your question. When you ask as if someone else wants to know, the answer is always NO. That's because I only consider requests that are delivered by the person who really wants to know. So if it's Jackson who wants to know, the answer is NO." With these words, specific and descriptive, Armand's father made it clear what behavior was inappropriate and the results that would follow.

Likewise, his next verbal choice indicated a clear and precise behavior that would work. He told Armand, "If you want me to consider the question seriously, you need to begin your question with an "I" statement. Say, "I want to know if I can stay overnight at Jackson's this Friday."

For maximum effect, create a clear picture on the front and back ends of your communication of what will and what will not work, what is appropriate and what is not.

Situation VI

Brenda began biting people when she was two years old. She occasionally bit other children at the day care center, bit her brother twice, and recently, in the middle of an angry tantrum, bit her mother.

Time-outs, raised voices, and threats failed to change Brenda's unacceptable behavior. When her dad learned about the One-Minute Behavior Modifier, he decided to use it to influence his daughter's biting.

Immediately following the verbal explosion of Brenda's

four-year-old brother and examination of the teeth marks on his arm, her dad launched his planned action. "Brenda, that is biting. Biting is not allowed in our home because it hurts people. Teeth are for chewing food and biting on a rubber toy only. When you are mad at your brother, stomp your feet like this [demonstration] and say, "No!""

Brenda practiced the new behavior twice while her father observed. Four more incidents of biting occurred before Brenda learned to stomp her feet as a way to let those around her know she was angry.

When Brenda's father was informed by a concerned day care supervisor that Brenda had started stomping her feet at other children, he smiled to himself, knowing that his efforts to eliminate biting had been successful.

If the behavior you are working on is one that is manifesting in different arenas, inform the other adults. Talk to the teacher, grandparent, day care worker, coach, scout leader, babysitter, piano teacher, or other parent. Give them advance warning of what you are doing and why you are doing it. Enlist their cooperation if possible.

Recommend this book or purchase a copy for their use. After all, it's your child, and the more people you have working in cooperation with your objectives the greater your chance of being successful.

Situation VII

Fred and Paul are brothers. They are three years apart in age, Fred being the oldest, now nine years old. They have pedal carts that they operate up and down the long drive-way that leads from the road up to their house and horse ranch.

Fred, being older, can go faster and make more intricate maneuvers with his pedal cart than his younger brother can. Fred gets much enjoyment from bumping his brother's cart and cutting him off by pulling in front of him. Paul gets frustrated and Fred enjoys that even more.

In an effort to control sibling rivalry and teach the values that are important to her family, the boy's mother implemented the One-Minute Behavior Modifier. "Fred, that's cutting your brother off," she said when she observed the behavior. "That's not helpful here because it slows him down. He can't pedal as well when you cut him off and he becomes unsuccessful. That makes it no fun for him. What would be helpful is for you to keep going fast so that you can both be successful."

In this case, the mother is attempting to craft a win/win solution for both her sons. She wants to insure that the younger one feels successful and enjoys riding the pedal cart. At the same time, her suggested new behavior helps the older son to have fun without infringing on the enjoyment of the younger brother.

Situation VIII

Ray is a teenage boy who visits his father on alternate week-ends. The father is more lax than his former spouse when it comes to discipline issues. He appears to have few, poorly enforced rules of behavior at his home.

Re-entry into the mother's home after a weekend with the father is creating problems between Ray and his mother. Ray resents the restrictions at his mother's and comes back angry. His anger often takes the form of cussing.

"Ray, that's cussing," his mother tells him. "Cussing is not permitted here because cuss words have a vulgar ring to them and do not respect me as a woman and as your mother. In addition, they are not necessary to get my attention. The way to get me to listen to your concerns is to use non-cussing words. If you're really angry and want to know why, you can write it all down any way you want and go back and cross out the cuss words. If you do that, I'll read it thoroughly and respond."

Ray's mother is at a disadvantage here. She is paying for the behavioral patterns of the father. Because he allows cussing and has few rules of behavior, she is forced to take the brunt of Ray's anger.

Cussing could be eliminated faster if both parents worked in tandem to affect the undesirable behavior. That's not going to happen in this instance, so this parent will have to work over a longer period of time to get the results she desires. She can expect periodic reverting to the cussing behavior by her teenager because the consistency that is needed is not fully present.

Situation IX

Fourteen-year-old Eric was a master at delivering vicious put-downs to other family members. "That's stupid," he would tell his sister. "You're dumber than rocks," he once told his younger brother, reducing him to tears. A few of his favorite expressions were:

"You're an idiot."
"You're sneakier than snake oil."
"You are one ugly duck."
"Ask me if I care."
"You call that intelligent?"
"I think your sense of humor just flew out the window."

In an effort to remove the divisiveness from his family, protect his other children, and help Eric learn a kinder, more appropriate behavior, Eric's father turned to the One-Minute Behavior Modifier. He knew that his son's verbal insults were different than teasing. His comments were verbal violence that sometimes led to physical violence in his family. So "verbal violence" is the name he chose to use when he delivered his well-thought-out verbal statement.

"Eric, that is verbal violence," this concerned father stated when he heard Eric call his sister "retarded". "We don't use verbal violence in this family because it puts other people down and destroys connectedness and trust. If you're angry or frustrated with your sister, tell her how you're feeling and what you would like to have happen. It might sound like this, "Cherry, I get really frustrated when you giggle so much. I'd like it if you could keep that under control at the dinner table.""

Eric thought his dad's request was stupid, so the verbal violence continued. So did use of the One-Minute Behavior Modifier. Eric's father used the technique in a variety of situations over several months. The behavior did not improve significantly.

So what if children don't stop the behavior when you use the One-Minute Behavior Modifier consistently? What if they just keep doing it? What do you do then?

Occasionally, one repetition of this verbal skill will be sufficient to end an undesirable behavior. Such was the case with Armand, in Situation V, who didn't take full responsibility for asking his questions. As soon as he heard his father's concern, Armand realized that the way he was asking wasn't going to get him what he wanted. When he was shown a new behavior, he had what appeared to be a spontaneous remission. He never reverted to the old behavior again. Behavior change can happen that quickly.

More often it takes several repetitions of the One-Minute Behavior Modifier before children learn you are serious. If you tell them whining doesn't work with you, be prepared to prove it, because your children will test you. Whining has worked so well for them for so long that they don't immediately trust your words. This is an important time in the process. It is critical that you demonstrate by your behavior that whining will never work with you again and continue to teach behaviors that do work.

Occasionally, you will find that no matter how many times you send your verbal statement, the child will not respond appropriately or will appear to forget it the next day. Such was the case with Eric. He continued to choose verbal violence as his way to demonstrate power and control in his family regardless of the careful teaching and sincere wishes of all his family members.

If you use the One-Minute Behavior Modifier consistently over time and get minimal results, it is time to move on. Chapter Two, "The Dynamic Discipline Equation," is specifically designed to help you move to the next level with a reluctant child. It contains a series of verbal strategies that help children see the connection between the choices they make and the results which follow. It is a discipline technique that will allow you to hold your children accountable for their behaviors and choices should they continue to choose inappropriate behaviors despite your best parenting efforts.

More help is just a page away. Read on.

Chapter Two

THE DYNAMIC
DISCIPLINE
EQUATION

Geoffrey Smith left home for college recently. He left prepared. He knows how to manage money, make choices, set goals, prioritize, work for what he wants, and survive in today's world. But more important, he takes responsibility for the choices he makes and accepts both the positive and negative consequences of his actions. He has both passion and purpose in place in his life. He is off on a grand adventure to create his future with intentionality. Geoffrey's parents have used the Dynamic Discipline Equation for several years with their son.

Robert Traxler is the same age as Andy. He lives across the street. He spends most of his days lying on the couch playing video games, eating cold pizza, and drinking diet soda. He does not take responsibility for the consequences of his actions and choices. He blames others for what happens to him. He thinks, talks, and acts like a victim. He has no direction, no mission, and no vision of his future. He hopes something good will happen to him some day. Robert's parents are unaware of the Dynamic Discipline Equation and the positive difference it can make in the lives of children.

Somewhere between the age of eighteen and twenty-five most children leave home. Like Geoffrey, some go away to college. Others join the service or the world of work. Still others go off to get married or simply move out to be on their own. Regardless of why or when, leaving home is part of the natural order. It happens to most children sooner or later.

Whenever children leave home, for whatever reason, our hope is that they can handle the experience successfully. We want them to leave with skills and a perspective that helps them see themselves as capable and responsible. We want them to approach life with attitudes of persistence, determination, and confidence. We want them to learn from their new experiences and continue to grow and evolve as mature human beings.

What is your goal in raising children? Do you want a thirty-year-old video-game player who leaves wet towels on the bathroom floor living at your house? Or is your desire to raise a young adult who functions successfully on his own with little input from you? Do you want someone who stops by to visit with the grandkids or someone who leaves the grandkids for you to raise on your own?

Think about what you want as the end product of eighteen to twenty-five years of raising a child. Our guess is that you want the result of your parenting efforts to be a responsible, capable, confident person, right? If so, it is important to learn and use the Dynamic Discipline Equation now.

Three words are all it takes to verbalize the Dynamic Discipline Equation:

Opportunity equals responsibility.

These three words can become the cornerstone of your family discipline policy. This important equation is a way to offer your children choices, a degree of control over their own lives, and an opportunity to learn about the relationship between cause and effect. It also provides you with a formula for holding your children accountable in a loving and respectful manner.

Let's take a closer look at the Dynamic Discipline

Equation in action.

Ivonne , a child of six, has the opportunity to play with Matchbox cars. She continues to earn the opportunity to play with them if she plays with them responsibly. "If you *choose* to throw them," her mother tells her, "you have *decided* to lose the opportunity to play with your cars for a while." Ivonne's mother believes and communicates that with opportunity comes responsibility. In her family, if the responsibility is taken seriously, the opportunity continues. If responsibility vanishes, so does the opportunity.

"You have the opportunity to ride your new bike all over the neighborhood," Beth Vogel told her eight-year-old son. "With this opportunity comes responsibility. Your responsibility is to wear a helmet at all times while you're riding. One of my main goals as a parent is to keep you safe, and a helmet will help me do that. If you *choose* to ignore the responsibility, you will be *choosing* to reduce your opportunity to ride your bike. If the responsibility is lessened, the opportunity will be lessened as well. If the responsibility stays strong, the opportunity will stay strong."

"Oops. I see you writing on the table with crayons," Mike Mason told his preschooler. "Crayons are for writing on paper. Here's some paper that we use with crayons. As long as you *choose* to use the crayons on the paper, you'll have the opportunity to continue using them. If you forget the responsibility and *choose* to use crayons on other surfaces, you will be *deciding* to give up the opportunity to use the crayons for a while."

Jason was given the opportunity to drive himself to

school. Since he was a new driver, his parents did not want the distraction of other teens in the car with their son while he was concentrating on driving. They explained it to him this way: "Jason, you have the opportunity to drive yourself to school. Your responsibilities include driving the speed limit and driving alone. As long as you handle those responsibilities well, you will continue to earn the opportunity to take the car on school days. If the responsibility is compromised, the opportunity will be altered as well. Remember, in our family opportunity equals responsibility."

Situation I

Katilina Jaurez is a single mom. Her two young boys are active, loud, and aggressive. They present a challenge to her parenting skills and attitude. Her biggest concern is Ozzie, her seven-year-old, who delights in hitting and kicking his younger bother.

"I made him sit in the naughty chair, took TV away from him, and yelled at him, but nothing worked," she told us at one of our Transformational Parenting workshops.

"I started using a behavior modification reward system that I heard about on the radio, but that only worked for a little while. He still kicks and hits. Recently, I spanked him. I don't like myself when I do that," she confessed. "I feel like a failure as a parent, but I get frustrated. I don't know what else to do."

Hitting little people to get them to stop hitting even smaller people makes no sense. It models the exact behavior you wish to eliminate. It teaches that might does indeed make right.

When you hit, yell, threaten, bribe, shame, or ridicule a child for not possessing the skills you want him to have, you are demonstrating that you don't have the skills they need you to have. You are as unskilled as they are.

In this case, when it came to dealing with the physical aggression of her son, Katilina was both unskilled and unaware of an effective alternative that would eliminate the hitting and kicking and help her see herself as a capable and loving parent. During her time at our workshop she learned the Dynamic Discipline Equation. After practicing it several times in simulated situations during the training, she felt ready to use it at home with her family.

At a family meeting one Sunday night Katilina told her children, "We are entering a new phase in our family. During this phase I'll be using some big words: "opportunity" and "responsibility." What it means is this: You will have many opportunities to do things you like. Most of them will have responsibilities that go with them. As long as you choose to accept the responsibilities, you will have the opportunity to continue. If you choose not to accept the responsibility, you will be choosing not to have the opportunity for a while.

"For example," she continued, "you have the opportunity to play in the front yard. Your responsibility is to stay in the front yard. If you choose to go outside of the fence, you will be choosing to lose that opportunity for a while. If you choose to stay in the yard, the opportunity to play outside will continue to be available to you."

"You have the opportunity to play with your trucks and race cars. Your responsibility is to put them away when

you're finished playing with them. If you choose to ignore the responsibility of putting them away, you will have chosen to lose the opportunity to play with them for a few days."

The boys listened to her explanation, asked no questions, and said they understood.

Later that night, Ozzie hit his brother with a plastic baseball bat. Katilina moved in quickly. After attending to Orestes and giving him the nurturing and attention he deserved, she turned to her older son. "Ozzie," she explained, "in our family opportunity equals responsibility. You have the opportunity to play with your brother. Your responsibility is to touch each other gently. If you choose not to do that, you choose to lose the opportunity to play with him. You will be deciding to play alone in your room. Do you understand?"

"I do," said the seven-year-old.

Ten minutes later Ozzie hit his brother again, this time with a wooden drum stick. His mother once again responded immediately. "Ozzie," she said, "when you choose not to accept the responsibility, you choose to lose the opportunity. You will now have a different opportunity, the opportunity to play alone in your room for a while."

She led the disgruntled youngster upstairs to his bedroom and explained the new options to him. "Can I have another chance?" he asked. "Yes," she answered, "in about forty-five minutes. At that time you'll have another opportunity to play with your brother. If you choose to accept the responsibility of playing gently at that time, you can play with him until bedtime. I'll be back."

Katilina then left the room, leaving Ozzie to play by himself.

Katalina's story illustrates the four important steps involved in using the Dynamic Discipline Equation.

1. Explain the opportunity that the child has and the responsibility that goes with it before you implement any consequences.

Katilina did just that when she told her son, "Ozzie, in our family opportunity equals responsibility. You have the opportunity to play with your brother. Your responsibility is to touch each other gently. If you *choose* not to do that, you *choose* to lose the opportunity to play with him. You will be *deciding* to play alone in your room. Do you understand?"

Notice that Katilina did not implement the outcome of playing alone the first time Ozzie he hit Orestes. To do so would have given him the consequence without his knowing in advance it was a possibility. When that happens, the child often sees the parent as the one responsible for his losing the opportunity. Katilina explained the entire equation to Ozzie and allowed him to choose again before any consequence was implemented. That put her son in charge of which outcome resulted and increased the chance that he would see himself as responsible for the result.

2. Allow the child to choose the behavior and thus the outcome which follows.

After explaining the Dynamic Discipline Equation, Katilina returned to her activities and assumed her children would play appropriately. She did not tell Ozzie what to do. She presented the choices and shared the possible outcomes wrapped neatly in the Dynamic Discipline Equation.

3. Follow through immediately by altering the opportunity. Give no second chance.

As soon as Ozzie hit Orestes, his mother went quickly to the area of the altercation. After attending to the recipient of the aggression, she turned to the perpetrator and reminded him of the equation and the outcome that his choice called for. Although he asked for a second chance, she gave none. He lost the opportunity to play with his brother.

4. Do give other opportunities to handle the responsibility later.

An hour later, this parent gave her son another opportunity to play with his brother. Her goal - to have her children play gently with each other - can only be practiced and learned when the boys are together. To keep them separated for long periods of time does nothing to help them learn how to play well together. That's why Ozzie needs and will be provided with as many opportunities to handle the responsibility as are necessary.

If Ozzie hits Orestes again, Katilina will move in again and resume the cycle at step three. She will follow through by reminding him that opportunity equals responsibility and that he has chosen to lose the opportunity again.

Situation II

Brandon Everman was having a problem with his teen driver. Emily, his daughter, was taking the car on weekend nights and returning it with an empty gas tank. Several conversations about the matter did little to affect the outcome. Despite the conversations and pleading, Emily regularly returned the car with less gas than it had when she took it.

Brandon decided to employ the Dynamic Discipline Equation.

"Can I take the car tonight, Dad?" Emily asked during Friday morning breakfast.

"Yep. Sure can," her father told her. "You have the opportunity to use the car tonight and any weekend night that I'm not using it. You also have the responsibility to return it with half a tank of gas or more. As far as this car goes, opportunity equals responsibility."

"What does that mean?"

"It means that if you choose to return the car with half a tank of gas or more, you have decided to use it again Saturday night. If you choose to return the car with less than half a tank of gas, you have decided not to use it tomorrow night. There is a responsibility that goes with the opportunity to use my car. If you handle the responsibility well, the opportunities will keep on coming. If not, the opportunities will dwindle. How often and how much the opportunities dwindle depends on you and the choices you make concerning the gas responsibility."

"Why are you doing this?"

"So you can be in charge of how often you take my car and so there is gas in it when I need it in the morning."

"Oh."

"Do you understand?"

"I think so."

"How about saying it back to me so we can both be sure that our understanding of the situation is the same." Emily then gave a perfect paraphrase of the "opportunity equals responsibility" speech her father had made moments before.

The next morning Brandon jumped in the car to go get a newspaper and a doughnut and noticed the gas gauge was below half. It wasn't a lot below half, but the arrow clearly indicated that the tank was less than half full.

When Emily entered the family room later that morning, her father stated calmly, "I see you chose not to have the car tonight."

"What do you mean, I chose not to have the car tonight?" Emily shot back.

"You know our deal about gas. If you choose to return the car with half a tank of gas or more, you've decided to use it again Saturday night. If you choose to return the car with less than half a tank of gas, you've decided not to use it. I noticed the gas gauge was below half." Brandon suspected a flurry of defensiveness and begging would follow, but he was determined to follow the guidelines of the Dynamic Discipline Equation and give no second chance. He resolved to remain firm and calm.

"Dad, I didn't notice that I needed gas until it was real late. You're always telling me to be home on time. I didn't have time to do both. You have to make up your mind. Do you want me home on time or do you want gas in the car?"

"I want both."

"Dad, please? I promised my friends I would drive tonight. I'll go fill it up right now."

"Sorry, no."

"What if I wash the car, too? It's really important to me."

"Nope."

"Dad, you're not being fair. There isn't another parent in the whole neighborhood who would do this to their kid."

"You're probably right."

"Can I take it then?"

"Sorry."

Emily then turned and stomped up the stairs and closed her door loudly as she entered her room.

Brandon did not follow. Instead of letting himself get hooked into turning the situation into an extended argument about slamming doors, he returned to the garage to finish a project he had begun the night before.

Brandon Everman demonstrated a classic rendition of the Dynamic Discipline Equation. He spelled out the equation and its implications before he limited car driving privileges. He did not cave in when his daughter whined, told him he was unfair, made excuses, or pouted. He gave no second chance and, much to her chagrin, she did not get the car that night.

In addition, Brandon did not make his daughter wrong. He did not make her bad. He did not make her cheap, forgetful, lazy, or irresponsible. He simply made her someone who didn't get the car that night. And he did it with love in his heart.

The following weekend Brandon Everman gave Emily a second opportunity. He created an identical proposition. He told her, "You can take the car tonight. Remember, opportunity equals responsibility. You have the opportunity to use the car this evening. Your responsibility is to put gas in it. If you choose to put gas in the car you're choosing to have it tomorrow night. If you choose not to, you're choosing not to have it tomorrow night." Then he stood back, let her choose, and once again gave her whatever consequence she asked for.

If Emily puts gas in the car, it's perfect. Brandon doesn't have to do it and he can feel good that his daughter is learning about following through on responsibilities. If she doesn't put gas in the car, it's perfect. It's the perfect opportunity for him to demonstrate for his daughter that her choices have outcomes that affect her life. Brandon is prepared to repeat this same process as many times as is necessary. Once again, he will give no second chance, and he is prepared and willing to extend many opportunities.

Holding Children Accountable

The Dynamic Discipline Equation is an important and foundation-building ingredient of a successful discipline strategy. One critical piece - the glue that holds it all together, the key to helping children choose appropriate behaviors and learn responsibility - lies in consistently holding them accountable for their actions and choices.

Holding children accountable means following through with what you said you were going to do. If you tell a child the responsibility that goes with the opportunity to be off with his friends is to be home on time, you need to follow through with the arrangement you set up. If you tell him, "If you choose to be home late you're choosing to spend the next evening with the family," and he comes home late, it is critical that he spends the next evening with his family. Give no second chance.

If you tell your daughter, "If you choose to clean up your room you're choosing to have an overnight guest," and she doesn't clean up her room, guess what? That's right, no overnight guest.

Holding children accountable for their actions is one of the most loving things you can do as a parent. It's a way of telling your children *I care about you.* Do you care enough about your children to set limits and design consequences that flow naturally from the choices they make concerning those limits? Do you love them enough to follow through with the outcomes those behaviors call for?

At times, some parents feel it is easier to cave in than

to hold the line where consequences are concerned. At first glance, it seems easier to let your son have one more chance at putting his hockey equipment where it belongs than to listen to him complain about not having it for the impromptu street hockey game that his friends have just organized. It feels like a loving thing to do to give your daughter ten dollars for a movie that all the other kids are going to when she's already spent this week's allowance. It seems like you're helping your child by running the forgotten band instrument to school when he calls and promises never to forget it again.

You're not helping if you engage in this kind of behavior. Helping doesn't always help. Sometimes it creates learned helplessness. The lesson children learn from not being held accountable is: If I come up with good excuses, if I create a scene, if I pout and whine, if I'm extra polite and sincere, if I beg in a parent-pleasing way, I can delay and often eliminate consequences. I don't have to be responsible for my own behaviors. Mom or Dad will bail me out.

You might indeed be bailing your children out - out of jail if you don't hold them accountable for the choices they make when they are young. Eventually, someone will hold your children accountable. If not you, the school will. If not the school, the police will. If not the police, the universe will. Wouldn't you rather have the person holding your children accountable be the one who knows them best, the one who loves them the most? Wouldn't you like to have that done when the stakes are small and the price they have to pay is insignificant? Do it now.

The Three Rs of Consequences

Using the Dynamic Discipline Equation is a systematic way to extend your parental love by empowering your children with age-appropriate choices and by implementing the natural outcomes that flow from those choices.

A consequence is not a punishment. It is simply a byproduct of an earlier choice. It can be either a positive or a negative outcome, depending on the behavioral choice of the child. If a consequence is too severe, is unconnected to the behavior, or is delivered with disrespect, it will come across as punishment rather than as an outcome of a choice. Using the Dynamic Discipline Equation is a fail-safe way to make sure your consequences are seen as outcomes rather than as punishments. The equation will help you construct meaningful outcomes that are *related, reasonable,* and delivered in a *respectful* manner.

1. Make consequences *relate* to the behavior.

If your son spills milk at the dinner table and is required to do all the dishes after dinner, there is no clear connection between the action and the result which followed. The outcome is not related to the behavior. If your daughter has to stay in the house for the weekend because she left her books at school, there is no real link from the behavior to the consequence that helps her see clearly the connection between the cause and the results which follow.

If a consequence is unrelated to the behavior, it is more likely to be interpreted in the child's mind as punishment. The child's focus is then likely to be on the person administering the punishment rather than on his or her choice of behavior. Children in these situations are likely to focus on the parent and what is being "done" to them rather than thinking about what they can learn from the situation and what they might choose to do differently next time.

Examples of related consequences:

- *Spill milk at the dinner table:* Clean it up, practice pouring milk over the sink after dinner.

- *Leave your books at school:* Pay your parent to drive you there. If the school is closed, create a written plan on how you will remember books next time. Make up all work the following week.

- *Regularly forget to feed the fish and clean the fish bowl:* Lose the opportunity to have fish.

- *Wet your bed:* Put wet sheets and clothes in the washer before you go to school. Put them in the dryer as soon as you come home. Take them out and make your bed when they're dry.

- *Leave your band instrument at home:* Go to band class without it and create a written plan for how you will remember it the next band day.

- *Get a speeding ticket:* Pay the ticket and all increases on your parent's insurance. Lose the opportunity to operate the car for a week.

2. Design *reasonable* consequences.

Some parents search for a consequence that will be strongly felt. It's as if they feel if the consequence hurts in some way, or induces fear, the child will retain the lesson. We disagree. It is not the severity of a consequence that has the impact, it is the certainty. Reasonable consequences delivered with absolute certainty allow children to trust the structure. For children to experience the full flavor of the cause and effect relationship of their choices and the outcomes which flow from those choices, you must be consistent in implementing the consequences.

Examples of reasonable consequences:

• Behavior: Throwing sand

Reasonable: *Losing the opportunity to play in the sandbox for two hours.*
Not reasonable: *Losing the opportunity to play in the sandbox for a week.*

• Behavior: Not putting your bike away

Reasonable: *Losing the opportunity to ride your bike for two days.*
Not reasonable: *Losing the opportunity to ride your bike for two weeks.*

• Behavior: Coming home after curfew

Reasonable: *Spending the next evening with your family. (Children call it "being grounded.")*
Not reasonable: *Spending every evening for a month with your family.*

• Behavior: Disrespectful communication

Reasonable: *Creating a plan for talking to your grand-*

mother differently next time and making amends.
Not reasonable: *Mowing her grass for the summer.*

Remember, one goal of using the Dynamic Discipline Equation "opportunity equals responsibility" is to help children learn how to make a different choice next time. If the consequence is severe, unexpected, or of inappropriate duration, the learning opportunity is likely to be lost as the person involved is caught up in feelings of anger and hurt.

3. Deliver consequences in a *respectful* manner.

In addition to consequences needing to be both related to the behavior and reasonable, they need to be delivered in a respectful manner. When informing children of the outcome of their actions, set your angry feelings aside. If you don't, they will tune into your anger and focus on your emotion rather than on the real message you are attempting to deliver.

Speak calmly, firmly, and seriously when you announce, "I see you decided to spend the evening with your family," or "I saw sand above the waist. That means you've chosen a different opportunity than playing in the sandbox." When you keep irritation, annoyance, or anger out of your communication about the outcomes of your child's choice, you can stay centered. This will allow you to concentrate on teaching rather than on punishing.

Refrain from using words that attack character or personality. Instead, use words that speak to the situation. "Pretty stupid choice on your part" attacks character. "When you choose to get a D you choose to have a tutor the next marking period" talks about the situation. "That was ridiculous on your part" is about character. "When you make that choice, you have also chosen to lose the opportunity to use that material for two days" focuses on the behavioral choice.

Speak to the situation with resolve and a tone that reflects serious concern but not catastrophe. Spilled milk is not the end of the world. Neither is mud on the living room floor or wet towels left in the bathroom. The sun will still come up tomorrow regardless of the amount of sand that gets tracked into the garage.

Listen as well as speak. You are likely to hear defensiveness, excuses, pleading, promising, bribing, whining, crying, and other manipulative moves from your children to get you to change your mind. Listen and help them realize you understand their concerns. And remember, understanding does not mean agreeing. Stay firm in your resolve to follow through with the consequences they have earned.

Situation III

Michelle Fivensen, age eleven, developed the habit of leaving dirty dishes in her bedroom. The result of that choice was an influx of ants who discovered the leftover food treasures and invited a full parade of their friends to join the feast.

The strategy of continually reminding, threatening, rewarding, yelling, reprimanding, pleading, and nagging did not produce the desired behavior change. It rarely does.

At the time, Michelle's parents, who were concerned about several issues with their four children, were talking regu-

larly with Chick, whom they had employed as their parent coach. Four weeks into their formal coaching sessions, Chick taught them the Dynamic Discipline Equation, which he recommended they use in dealing with several family situations. Saul Fivensen immediately recognized this strategy's potential for use with Michelle's failure to return dirty dishes to the proper place.

After being exposed to the technique, he didn't wait long to implement it. "I want to support you in your desire to take snacks to your room," he told his daughter, "and I'm concerned about ants in our home. From now on, in regard to snacks, opportunity equals responsibility. You have the opportunity to take popcorn, ice cream and other treats to your room on approved occasions, and you have the responsibility to bring the dishes back to the kitchen and place them in the sink. Opportunity and responsibility go hand in hand. One cannot exist without the other. If the responsibility is neglected, the opportunity to have snacks in your room will be lost. If the responsibility is accepted, the opportunity will remain. Do you understand?"

Michelle said she did, and her father checked for understanding by having her restate the relationship between opportunity and responsibility in her own words. Upon conclusion of her explanation, both father and daughter were satisfied that they shared a mutual understanding of the situation.

Friday night of that same week Michelle's best friend was scheduled to spend the night. Friday morning, after Michelle had left for school, Mr. Fivensen found dirty dishes in her bedroom. When he got home from work that evening, he informed her, "Michelle, I found an ice cream bowl and spoon in your room this morning. Since you chose

to make the responsibility a low priority, you have also created a loss of opportunity to have food in your room this
weekend. The opportunity to have food in your bedroom will
be restored on Sunday night." His words prompted the following conversation.

"Daddy, I just forgot. I'll take care of it right now."

"I already cleaned it up this morning. I didn't want it to
attract ants."

"I won't do it again. I promise."

"I believe you, and you'll have a chance to demonstrate that
beginning Sunday night."

"Daddy, please. Madison is coming over tonight and we're
going to order pizza."

"That's a bummer. Pizza is fine and you will have to find
another place to eat it."

"But we want to eat it in my room."

"I know. That would have been fun. It's really too bad.
You'll have to do that another time."

"This isn't fair."

"I know it seems unfair to you. To me it fits the equation we
live by in this house: opportunity equals responsibility."

"You're being mean."

"I know it looks mean to you and I can see how you think
that. And I'm not going to change my mind on this one."

"What if I clean the whole house?"

"Sorry, nope."

"And wash your car?"

"Nope."

"You're impossible."

"You're probably right."

Saul Fivensen exhibited several strengths as he guided his daughter and himself through this valuable learning experience.

1. He laid out the expectations and possible ramifications ahead of time using the Dynamic Discipline Equation.
2. He checked for understanding.
3. He set it up so that his daughter was responsible for the outcome.
4. He stayed calm when he explained the situation and the resulting consequences.
5. The consequence was related, reasonable, and communicated with respect.
6. He listened more often than he spoke.
7. He communicated empathy when she explained the situation.
8. He did not attack her character or personality.
9. He did not cave in and gave her no second chance.
10. He told her when she would have another opportunity.

Dirty dishes in the bedroom diminished significantly after the above incident. Only once in the six months that followed did Michelle fail to handle her responsibility of returning dishes to the kitchen. When that occurred, her father again followed through immediately, implementing the Dynamic Discipline Equation, which by then he had been successfully using in dealing with several other family situations.

Saul Fivensen's successful handling of the dirty dishes in the bedroom caper did not happen by luck, magic, or circumstance. It did not happen because he bribed, punished, or created fear in his daughter. He was successful because he developed skills that work, learned how to place the responsibility for outcomes on his daughter, and delivered his verbal communication and the consequences with love and an open heart.

The Cause and Effect Connectors

Three special words - *choose, decide, and pick* - will help you add meaning and strength to the Dynamic Discipline Equation. They are important linking words that help children see the connection between cause and effect. These three words will help your children become decisive, empowered, and increasingly responsible and confident. If used early and often with your children, they will lay a helpful foundation for effective discipline moves when they reach their teen years.

"Choose," "choosing," "chose," "chosen," "chooser," "decide," "deciding," "decided," "decider," "pick," "picker," "picked," and "picking" are all appropriate cause and effect connectors that will help your child become the responsible adult you wish to create.

Use choose/decide/pick with consequences.

- "If you choose to play quietly, you have *decided* to stay here with me in the kitchen."

- "If you *choose* to be in chat rooms on the computer, you will be *deciding* not to use the computer for two days."

- "When you *choose* to throw food from your high chair, you *choose* to be done eating and get down."

- "When you *choose* that type of language in our home, you have *chosen* to create a written plan to eliminate that behavior."

For children to understand the relationship between cause and effect, consequences must follow their choices and behaviors. Use choose/decide/pick in your parent talk to connect the consequence to the behavior. When you do that, you help your children experience the cause and effect nature of their choices and the results that follow.

- "If you decide to be home on time, you have chosen to visit your friends again tomorrow."

- "When you choose to throw your toys, you decide to have them on the shelf for the rest of the day."

- "If you choose not to call us on the cell phone when your plans change, you will be deciding not to have a cell phone for three days."

When using the cause and effect connectors of choose/decide/pick, be sure to use them on both sides of the equation.

"If you choose not to be home on time, I won't let you go out tomorrow night" uses a connector on only the first side of the equation. It sends a different message than "If you choose not to be home on time, you've *decided* not to go out tomorrow night."

"If you decide not to complete your school work at school, I'll keep you in on Saturday" creates a vastly different impression than "If you decide not to complete your school work at school, *you will have chosen* to do it on Saturday."

When you use choose/decide/pick on both sides of the equation, children learn over time that they are in control of the outcome. It puts them in charge of which results follow.

When you say, "If you decide not to complete your school work at school, I'll keep you in on Saturday," and then follow through, the child sees you as being responsible for his staying in on Saturday. If your parent talk is, "If you decide not to complete your school work at school, *you will have chosen* to do it on Saturday," and you follow through, there is a greater chance he will see himself as responsible for how he spends his Saturday.

If you say, "When you choose to throw your toys, I'm putting them on the shelf for the rest of the day," it hurts the child from the outside in. It is *you* doing it to her. She looks to you as the source of discomfort. On the other hand, if your parent talk is, "When you choose to throw your toys, you *decide* to have them on the shelf for the rest of the day," she hurts from the inside out. It is her doing it to herself. She is more likely to see herself as the source of her pain.

This parenting strategy asks you to structure your behavior and your language in such a way that the child gets to be the cause of the outcomes he creates in his life. Using the cause and effect connectors to attach a behavior to a consequence is a discipline strategy that puts the child in charge of which outcomes occur.

In the following examples, who do you feel is the cause of the outcome?

- "If you *choose* to bring the car back with more than half a tank of gas, you will be *choosing* to use it again tomorrow night. If you *decide* to bring it back with less than half a tank of gas, you will be *deciding* not to use it tomorrow night."

Who gets to be the cause of whether or not this teen gets to use the car tomorrow? The teen does. She creates her own conditions based on the choices she makes. She is the creator of her present reality.

- "If you *choose* to leave your study materials at school, you will be *choosing* to pay me to take you there to get them."

Who is the cause of determining if this child pays for Mom's taxi service to school? This child is. He has control of whether or not he brings his study materials home and the results which follow. It is his choice.

"Coming home late is not a choice in my family," a father told us recently at one of our parenting workshops. "So I don't give choices around issues of that kind." This father misses one important fact. Even if he tells his child to be home on time, posts rules, and reminds the child before she leaves, she still chooses whether or not to comply. Children do choose, even if you attempt to do their thinking for them and tell them what to do. They choose whether or not to go along with your wishes or demands. And since they really are the one who chooses to comply or not, why not use parent talk that reflects that reality instead of pretending you are the one doing the choosing?

Overuse choose/decide/pick.

Children don't usually see the cause and effect connection the first time you use "choose," "decide," and "pick." It often takes many repetitions before they understand and begin using the language themselves. Overuse these words. Use them more than you normally would. Use them more often than you think is necessary.

If you go to bed at night and you aren't thinking, "Man, am I sick and tired of using choose/decide/pick," you're not using them enough. When you inform your spouse, "I'm so sick of saying choose/decide/pick," hang in there. That's exactly where you need to be.

"My kids don't understand words like choose, decide, and pick," a mother told us in the middle of one of our training programs. "They're too young to grasp a concept like choosing."

If your children don't understand "options," "decision," and "choice," it's because you don't use those words around them often enough. Children learn words that are spoken in their presence. They expand their vocabulary and understanding of words through the use of those words by the important people in their lives. Use the word "choose" in the presence of a young child twenty times and that child will understand the meaning, as well as what is likely to follow.

We recommend that you use the equation "opportunity equals responsibility" with children as young as three years of age. Of course, they don't know those words when you first start using them. They will after several repetitions. Young children don't understand the word "no" when they first hear it. And it doesn't take them long to figure it out, does it? The same phenomenon will occur with "responsibility" and "opportunity."

Situation IV

After reading one of our articles on our website, Ichiro Shingo informed his teen, "If you choose to be home by ten o'clock, you've decided to spend some time with your friends tomorrow night. If you choose to be home after ten o'clock, you've decided to spend tomorrow evening with your family."

"You mean I'm grounded?" the teen inquired.

"We don't call it grounded," replied the father. "We call it choosing to spend the evening with your family."

"I'm grounded," said the son. He then turned and walked away.

Even when you use the cause and effect connectors, as Ichiro did, children don't always see themselves as responsible. Often, their initial reaction is to dodge responsibility and perceive you as the one who is doing it to them. Ichiro's son sees his father as the person doing the grounding at this point. It may take many repetitions of using the cause and effect connectors before this teen understands the connection and the role he plays in creating the outcomes. Be persistent and consistent with your use of this important discipline technique.

Your Attitude Matters

The attitude you bring to implementation of the Dynamic Discipline Equation and use of the cause and effect connectors is critical. We suggest you adopt two critically important attitudes as you implement the ideas in this chapter. We recommend that you *don't care* and *see it all as perfect.*

Don't care?

Yes, don't care.

If you give your child a choice of using the red cup or the blue cup, *don't care* what cup he picks. If the decision is to do schoolwork before or after dinner, *don't care* if your daughter chooses to do it before dinner. Likewise, *don't care* if she chooses to do it after dinner.

Tell your son, "Opportunity equals responsibility.

Your opportunity is to have some goldfish to enjoy and care for. Your responsibility is to feed the fish every night and clean the bowl once a week." Then *don't care* whether he follows through or not.

Explain to your daughter, "Opportunity equals responsibility. You have the opportunity to use the car tonight. Your responsibility is to put gas in the tank before you come home." Then *don't care* whether she puts gas in the tank or not.

How can we say, "Don't care?," you might be wondering.

We don't care because we *see it all as perfect.*

If your daughter puts gas in the car, it's perfect. You don't have to, and she is learning to be responsible and to handle her obligations honorably. If she fails to put gas in the car, it's still perfect. It's the perfect opportunity to help her learn what happens when she chooses not to put gas in the car, the perfect opportunity to help her learn about the connection between cause and effect. In fact, you can't find a more perfect opportunity to help her learn that lesson.

If your son feeds the fish and cleans out the fishbowl regularly, it's perfect. He's learning about caring for another living thing and the responsibility that comes with that. If he fails to feed the fish and clean the fishbowl regularly, it's perfect. Once again, it is the perfect time to help him see what happens if he chooses not to take the responsibility that is his. It is the perfect time for him to receive a lesson on the connection between opportunity and responsibility.

When you see it all as perfect, you do not become emotionally invested in which choice your child selects. You don't care. And since you don't care, you won't get excessively upset when he or she doesn't select your preferred choice. That's because you no longer have a preferred choice. You don't have a pre-ferred choice anymore because you realize it's all per-fect and that the perfect lesson will be delivered regardless of the choice your child makes.

But what about getting mad? you may wonder. Doesn't every parent get frustrated, annoyed, and irri-tated with children from time to time?

Yes, we all do. Kids do annoying, frustrating, irritating things sometimes. And even though we strongly sug-gest you stay centered and calm when using the Dynamic Discipline Equation, and even choose not to care what choice your children make, we're not going to tell you never to get angry or upset. In fact, we think that hiding anger and annoyance often does children a disservice.

Children need to know when we are angry and upset. The trick is to learn the necessary verbal skills that will enable you to communicate that anger in a way that does not wound their spirit, in a way that does not attack character, in a way that allows children to keep their dignity intact. To do that, we move to Chapter Three, "The Positive Anger Explosion."

Chapter Three

THE POSITIVE
ANGER EXPLOSION

Kids spill things, make messes, whine, talk inappro-
priately, choose behaviors that violate the family
norms, and challenge limits. They get sick, track in
mud, lose their mittens, refuse to eat certain foods,
and tease their siblings. They stay out past curfew, talk
back, and don't always do as well in school as we'd
like. And that's all on the first day of the week.

Guess what? Kids are going to do annoying, irritating,
frustrating things. That's what kids do. It's as if it's
written in their job description or encoded in their
genes.

Your children are going to do *their* job. One of *our* jobs
is to respond to those behaviors. A typical parental
response to unappreciated behaviors is anger, or one
of the variations of anger that include irritation,
annoyance, frustration, or disgust. Sometimes the
response is stifled anger. In some households, the
reaction is an explosion of pure rage.

What do you do when your child chooses a behavior
that can be interpreted as annoying? Do you get upset
or angry? If so, you fit in with the vast majority of parents. We can't think of a single parent who has not
been frustrated or upset with a child on one occasion
or another.

The important question is not, do you get upset and
impatient with children. Most everyone does. The real
issue is what do you do with those feelings, and if you
choose to express them, how skillfully do you do that?

When children choose behaviors that we see as annoying and we feel our irritation thermometer rising, we
have two choices. We can push the feelings down and

pretend they don't exist, or we can express them verbally.

The first choice - push the feelings down and pretend they don't exist - doesn't work. If you think you aren't communicating your irritation or your frustration when you attempt to numb it out, you are wrong. Your feelings are being broadcast and received non-verbally. Your children can tell when you're annoyed even if you attempt to push the feeling down and remain silent.

Although your children pick up the silent vibrations that reveal your feelings, they do miss something of utmost importance. They fail to learn specific and clarifying details of your feelings and are then left to guess at their origin. Lacking concrete and accurate information about parents' feelings, children often make false interpretations of the signals they think they're getting. Your silence forces them to guess about your feelings, and they base those guesses on incomplete data that is further confounded because it's being interpreted by an immature mind.

Another problem with pushing your feelings down is that you can only do that for so long before the pressure builds up and you explode. When the emotional explosion does occur, it usually happens over some relatively minor occurrence. Your children are then left to ponder why you got so excited about a minor event. An additional complication is that your explosion gives them more reason to look at you than to look inwardly for answers and responsibility.

When we choose not to express irritation, annoyance, and frustration, we do our children a disservice. They deserve to know that some of the behaviors they choose are adversely affecting the people around them. To encourage or help children to make alternative choices in the future it is necessary for us to communicate clearly and cleanly our feelings about their behavior in the present.

For these reasons, we advocate option two, expressing your feelings verbally. That's what Robert Logan did in the situation that follows.

Situation I

Monica's father felt his annoyance level rise when he saw his tools spread out on the front lawn. Monica knows these tools need to be put away when she's done using them, *he thought to himself as he parked the car and headed inside to find his twelve-year-old daughter.* I've told her that at least a dozen times.

When Mr. Logan located his daughter on the couch in front of the TV, he immediately made his feelings known. "What's the matter with you?" *he asked her.* "Do you think you can just use my good tools and leave them all over the lawn? Do you have any idea how much those tools cost? They cost a lot of money, and when you get a job someday you'll realize that. You make me so mad. Now get your lazy butt off the couch and show some responsibility with my tools. Hang them up in the garage where they belong."

The frustrated parent then turned and walked away, thinking he had encouraged responsibility in his daughter by effectively communicating his feelings.

He had not.

Although Mr. Logan chose to express his feelings, he did not do it skillfully. His communication style was one of attack. He attacked his daughter's character ("lazy butt"). He attacked her personality and shamed her ("Who do you think you are?"). He attacked her intelligence by doing her thinking for her ("Hang them up in the garage where they belong."). With his cut-and-slash approach to discipline, this father's words carried the high probability of wounding his daughter's spirit.

To insure that you express your anger cleanly, to make sure you don't wound your child's spirit, and to communicate in a respectful way, we recommend you use the *Positive Anger Explosion.*

The Positive Anger Explosion is a verbal technique designed to communicate frustration, irritation, annoyance, and other forms of anger without attacking personality or character. It is nonjudgmental, honest, and a clear message of your feelings. If used correctly, it guarantees that your language shows the same amount of respect you hope to elicit from the recipient.

The Anger Delivery Statement

The Anger Delivery Statement contains three important pieces. All three include a descriptive aspect of what you intend to communicate. When faced with a child's behavior and your rising emotion, do these three things:

    1. Describe the situation.

2. Describe how you are feeling.
3. Describe the desired outcome.

Consider the following scenario.

Situation II

Fernando Uribe found an empty juice box stuck between the cushions of his brand new couch. His six-year-old daughter, Marta, who had been snacking there earlier, was now upstairs in her room quietly reading.

As he made his way up the stairs to confront his daughter, Fernando could feel his irritation rising. When he got close to the door, he remembered the Positive Anger Explosion and its use for communicating strong emotion effectively. He paused for a moment outside her door, took a few deep breaths, constructed the three-part Anger Delivery Statement in his head, and then knocked on the door.

After being invited in, Fernando told his daughter directly and firmly, "Marta, I found an empty juice box in the couch. It's still there. I feel mad. Trash belongs in the garbage can under the sink."

With that he turned and walked away. A short time later, Marta made her way downstairs and took care of the juice box in an appropriate manner.

Let's take a closer look at Mr. Uribe's Positive Anger Explosion and the three descriptors his Anger Delivery Statement contains.

First, he described the situation. *"Marta, I found an*

empty juice box in the couch. It's still there." Notice that he did not talk about her memory, her level of responsibility, or any character trait. He talked only about the juice box and the couch. His words spoke only about the situation and did not once refer to his daughter.

Describing the situation is preferable to "Why can't you remember to keep the living room looking nice?," which points to a specific characteristic of the child. It certainly is an improvement on "You're such a slob. It looks like pigs live here," which is thinly veiled sarcasm that attacks the child's personality.

Next, Mr. Uribe described his feelings. *"I feel mad,"* this angry father told his young daughter. Notice that he wrapped his feelings in descriptive rather than accusatory language by using an "I" statement. He did not say, "You are irritating me," or "You are making me mad." He said, "I feel mad." Again, he chose not to talk about his daughter or point fingers. He spoke about himself by sharing what his internal reaction was to finding a juice box stuck in the couch. Our children deserve to get clear messages of parental feelings. Using "I" statements will help you do that.

An additional benefit of using the second descriptor is that it helps our children build their *feeling* vocabulary. Many children have limited feeling words in their vocabulary. If you ask them how they feel, they are likely to say *fine, good, OK, mad,* or *bad*. They do not have many words to choose from because they do not have adults in their lives who regularly use feeling words to describe their own feelings. When you use feeling words - *irritable, disgusted, annoyed, frustrated, exasperated, resentful, discouraged, depressed, impatient, irritated, flabbergasted* - you are helping your children by giving them access to the words they need to recognize and name their own feelings.

"Trash belongs in the garbage can under the sink" were the words Mr. Uribe used to conclude the trio of specific descriptions. His language focused only on describing the desired outcome. By doing so, he pointed to the solution rather than to the person who created the problem.

<u>Third, this father described the outcome he wanted.</u> Notice that he did not say, "Go put that juice box in the garbage can." He did not tell his daughter specifically what to do. Instead, he reminded her where trash belongs and trusted her to make a responsible choice. Your job is to describe what you want or need as an outcome. The child's job is to figure out what to do. This gives the child an opportunity to think, problem solve, and build positive character.

Examples of using the Positive Anger Explosion:

> *"Bucky, I noticed empty pop cans and candy wrappers in the back seat of the car after you returned it last night. I'm annoyed because it's not fun for me to drive a messy car. Pop cans and candy wrappers belong in the trash."*

> *"Tevi, I see dirty dishes on the dinner table. I feel resentful. Dirty dishes belong in the dishwasher after they're rinsed off."*

> *"Amanda, I found wet towels and a wet floor in the bathroom. My clean socks got soaked. I'm furious. Wet towels belong on the towel rack and the floor needs to be dry."*

> *"Brandon, I found ink stains and an ink pen in your school pants when they came out of the dryer. I'm exasperated because the pants are no longer available to be worn to school. Pants need to have empty pockets before they go in the washer."*

> *"Missy, I heard put-downs in your conversation with your sister. I'm discouraged and annoyed. Conversation in this family needs to be uplifting and affirming."*

When you describe the situation, what you are feeling, and what the desired outcome looks like, you achieve multiple benefits.

1. The problem is immediately identified.
2. You are giving children clear feedback about your strong feelings.
3. Accusations and personal attacks are eliminated.
4. The desired outcome is described without telling the child what to do, thus allowing him to think for himself.
5. The child has an opportunity to develop responsible behavior by determining how to respond to the situation.

Situation III

Paige's mother searched for her hairbrush for ten minutes so she could finish getting ready for work. By the time she found it in Paige's room the morning breakfast routine was behind schedule and the stress of having to play catch-up with the clock had kicked in. When Paige finished with her morning shower, she found her mother in an ornery mood.

"Paige, I found my hairbrush in your room under a pile of clothes. It took me a while to find it and now I'm running behind schedule. I'm feeling impatient. My hairbrush belongs in the same place I left it so it"s there when I need it."

"I'm sorry, Mom," responded the teen. "I got up late and was hurrying to get ready. I wish I had put it back last night after I got done using it. I'll do better next time."

"OK, now help me fix your sister's lunch, please."

"All right."

Paige's mother not only told her daughter how she was feeling in a clear and honest way, she also added an important component to her Positive Anger Explosion. She added a reason for her frustration: *"It took me a while to find it and now I'm running behind schedule."*

The reason given described how the missing hairbrush impacted the mother's life. This skilled parent chose language that contained the words *I* and *me*. With those words, the parent spoke only about herself and said nothing about her daughter. There is a big difference between, "It took *me* a while to find it and now *I* am running behind schedule," which tells only about the mother, and *"You* left it in a place that was hard to find and *you* have caused me to get behind schedule," which places blame on the child.

What If They Don't Do It?

"What if they don't do it?" is a question often asked at our parent workshops when we are leading an exercise to help parents learn and practice this valuable technique. It's usually posed by parents who can't envision their child returning the tools, removing the juice box from the couch, or taking care of the pop cans and candy wrappers in the back seat of the car regardless of how respectfully the frustration is communicated.

"It doesn't matter how skillfully I say it, my kid still doesn't do anything," one father told us. "The only thing that works with him is yelling and threatening to take away his electronic games." Our answer to that train of thought is simply this: We suggest you apply the following four questions to those strategies or to any discipline technique you decide to use.

1. Does it work?
2. Is it respectful?
3. Does it help you become the parent you
    always wanted to be?
4. What does it teach?

"If you can answer the first three questions affirmatively and are happy with your answer to question number four, then keep on yelling and threatening to take away a privilege," we told this father. His answer to question number one was "Sometimes." His answer to the next two questions was a resounding "No." He never articulated an answer to the final question.

The only question of the four that he could give a partial "yes" to was number one: Does it work? Even if yelling and threatening did work on occasion, we question the validity of that answer when applied to long-term results. Some parenting moves, such as threatening to remove a privilege, yelling, rewarding, shaming, dispensing guilt, or using physical punishment, can get the results you want short term. But at what cost and for how long?

Yelling and taking away electronic games might get your son to return the tools to their proper place in this one instance. But what about next time? Does the lesson carry over?

In our view, the lesson is more likely to be applied in future situations if you describe how you are feeling and communicate how the behavior affects your life. This helps children see that there is a cause and effect relationship between their choices and the impact those choices have on others. This increases the chance that they will make helpful, healthy choices not because *we* want them to, but because *they* want to, based on their own values and level of responsibility.

Regarding question two, yelling, threatening, and dispensing guilt are not respectful. Neither are bribing, shaming, or using physical punishment. And do these behaviors really help you become the parent you always wanted to be, as posed in question three? We think not.

Physical punishment (yes, that includes light spanking) teaches children that might makes right. It teaches that physical force is an appropriate way to get what you want in this world. Is that the lesson you want your children to learn? It is certainly not a lesson that we advocate teaching to youngsters. For more information on the issue of spanking, go to our Personal Power Press website, www.personalpower-press.com, and order the special report, *Spanking: "This is going to hurt me more than it hurts you."*

Giving rewards can bribe children into temporary compliance. But they learn that the only reason to do something is to get a reward. When you use this form of external control in your home, you deprive your children of opportunities to learn internal control. Also, you will have to create increasingly bigger rewards to get them to comply in the future. Again, more information on this topic can be found at www.personalpowerpress.com in our special report, *"Why is the teacher giving my kid M&M's?"*

When you yell to gain compliance, ask yourself, "What is my behavior teaching my children?" See if you like the answer. Then ask yourself, "Is this the parent that I really want to be?" Ponder the same questions when you shame, belittle, criticize, pout, lecture, scold, threaten, withhold love, or give your children the silent treatment.

Many times the Anger Delivery System works.

- It worked when Connie Wilson told her daughter, "Honey, your new jacket is on the floor. I'm feeling really frustrated. It belongs on a hook in the hall." Her daughter immediately hung up the jacket.

- When Gil Gilbert saw his son's goalie glove lying outside in the sleet and rain, he said,

"Jacques, I see your new goalie glove getting soaked outdoors in the driveway. I'm feeling discouraged. It seems to me like my money is going right down the drain. Hockey equipment belongs in the garage in the sports box where it can stay in tip-top condition." Jacques didn't wait to see what would happen next. He got up from the dinner table, retrieved the glove, and put it in the sports box.

- Chad Arrington found recently borrowed library books on the basement floor. After thinking carefully about his response, he said, "I see the books we just got at the library lying on the basement floor. I feel annoyed. Library books belong on the shelf so they don't get scraped and injured." His two preschoolers quickly scooted down the stairs and placed the books in their proper place.

When you describe what you hear or see, describe how you are feeling, and describe the desired outcome, as the parents above did, there is a good chance children will respond appropriately. Still, the Positive Anger Explosion technique is no guarantee that your child's behavior will match your desires. No parenting technique works every time with every child.

Situation IV

Casey Montgomery noticed baseball spikes and a baseball glove on the carpet of the family room. They belonged to his twelve-year-old daughter, Jenny, who was reading a book in the rocking chair nearby. Since Casey had spoken to Jenny about the baseball equipment and its proper place in this home (the garage) on several other occasions, he felt annoyance begin to well up inside. At this moment he chose to ignore the infraction, hoping his presence would serve as a friendly reminder and that Jenny would handle it on her own, without his intervention.

As the minutes slowly passed and Jenny made no effort to remove the baseball equipment from the family room, Casey's annoyance began to grow. Rather than waiting for it to peak, he decided to take action and use a Positive Anger Explosion.

"Jenny, I see your spikes and glove on the floor there by the big chair," he began, careful to describe exactly what he saw. "I'm feeling annoyed. Baseball equipment belongs on the shelf in the garage."

"I know," replied the youngster.

"Good," said Mr. Montgomery. "I just wanted to make sure you knew." With those words, he got up and departed the room, fully expecting his daughter to find an appropriate solution to the situation.

She did not.

Twenty minutes later Casey walked through the family room and found the baseball equipment still in the same place he had seen it before. His daughter had moved on to other projects in her bedroom.

So, you may be thinking, here is a classic case of the Positive Anger Explosion not working to produce the desired result.

Yes and no.

Yes, the desired result of having the baseball equipment removed from the family room was not achieved. That is correct and we will share how to handle that shortly.

But one other very important result was achieved. A major goal of the Positive Anger Explosion is to communicate anger in a way that does not wound the spirit or attack character. In that regard, Casey Montgomery was eminently successful. This goal was indeed realized. Do not assume that because the desired behavior didn't manifest, the statement was a failure. It was highly successful in achieving the result it was designed to produce: communicating anger in a clean, honest, and respectful way.

At this point, Casey had many options. He could . . .

1. Find his daughter and tell her to take care of the baseball equipment immediately.
2. Begin ranting and raving about responsibility and maturity.
3. Give her another gentle reminder.
4. Confine her to her room until she takes care of it.
5. Dispense shame by telling her how disappointed he is in her behavior.
6. Threaten to curtail her TV time if she doesn't handle her responsibilities.
7. Put a chart on the wall and have her make a mark when she completes a responsibility.
8. Mock her with sarcasm and clever remarks designed to show her that she didn't follow through.

9. Prevent her from playing in the Saturday
   morning baseball game.
10. Hide the equipment so she can't find it when
    she needs it.
11. Tell her again and start counting, "One, two,
    three . . ."

We recommend none of the above. Remember the four questions we suggested you ask yourself before you implement any discipline strategy.

1. Does it work?
2. Is it respectful?
3. Does it help you become the parent you
   always wanted to be?
4. What does it teach?

None of the listed options pass the four-question challenge. Most of them don't pass the first one.

At this point in the process it is time to implement one of the first two strategies described earlier. Both the One-Minute Behavior Modifier and the Dynamic Discipline Equation generate positive responses when put to the four-question test. Both are respectful. Both help you become the parent you always wanted to be. And both teach positive concepts to children. The One-Minute Behavior Modifier teaches the behavior you want to have the child substitute as an alternative to the unwanted behavior, and the Dynamic Discipline Equation teaches children that their choices produce outcomes and that they are in control of what those outcomes turn out to be.

Casey Montgomery can go to his daughter and implement the One-Minute Behavior Modifier, saying,

"Jenny, leaving your baseball gear in the family room is what we call ignoring the family limits. Ignoring the family limits is not something we do in this family because it creates problems for others and builds feelings of resentment. What we do in this family is respect the family limits. In this case that means keeping your possessions in their proper places."

Will this discipline strategy work? There's a good chance that it will. If not, another strategy, the Dynamic Discipline Equation, is waiting in the wings.

Is it respectful? It is if it's delivered in a polite tone and spoken as if this were the first time the behavior had ever occurred. Adding "Thanks for your cooperation" increases the respect level as well as the odds that the child will follow through with the desired behavior.

Does the One-Minute Behavior Modifier help you become the parent you always wanted to be? It does if you want to be a teacher to your children. It does if you want to be respectful. It does if you want to be a person who refuses to criticize, shame, or belittle.

What does it teach? It teaches that ignoring family limits has an adverse effect on family members, creating problems for them and building feelings of resentment. It teaches that the family members help each other with friendly reminders and take action immediately after the reminder. It teaches that respectful communication is the norm in this family. It teaches that people are treated with dignity no matter what choices they make. It teaches children how to be an effective parent when they grow up.

On those rare occasions when the child still chooses

not to follow through, employ the Dynamic Discipline Equation "opportunity equals responsibility." Using this option, Mr. Montgomery would go to his daughter and explain, "Jenny, in this family opportunity equals responsibility. You have the opportunity to play baseball and use the equipment we purchased recently. That includes your rubber-spiked shoes and your glove. Your responsibility is to keep them in the garage with the other sports equipment. If you choose to ignore the responsibility, you risk losing the opportunity to use them at a time when you might find them extremely helpful. You can let me know what opportunities you want by how you handle the responsibility."

How does this bit of parenting do in relation to the four questions? Will it work? Again, we think there is a good chance that it will. If not, there is still another strategy, *implementing consequences,* waiting to be used.

Is it respectful? It is if you speak calmly, firmly and seriously. It is if you keep irritation, annoyance, or anger from your communication as you deliver it. Not attacking character or personality is respectful. By speaking to the situation with resolve and in a tone that reflects serious concern but not catastrophe, you are respectful.

Does the Dynamic Discipline Equation help you become the parent you always wanted to be? That depends on who it is you want to be in your role of parent. If you want to be the policeperson who catches people being bad and hands out punishment, it does not. If you want to be the judge who determines if behavior is right or wrong and administers sentences, it does not. If you want to be the warden who enforces the punishment and guards to see that it is being carried out, it does not.

On the other hand, it does if you want to be the teacher. It does if you want to be a respectful parent. It does if you want to be honest, open, and direct in your communication style.

What does the Dynamic Discipline Equation teach? It teaches children that there is a cause and effect dynamic that operates in the universe. It teaches them they are in control of the outcomes they produce in their lives. It teaches them that if they don't like the outcomes their choices create, they can make different choices and alter those outcomes. It teaches them that they are empowered individuals capable of shaping their own destiny.

Suppose they still choose not to? Then what?

If children still choose not to change a behavior, and some youngsters do make that choice, it is time to implement the consequences they have chosen with consistency and an open heart. It's time to follow through with the related, reasonable, and respectful outcomes of their actions. It's time to love your child by giving her what she asked for.

Will that work? Yes, some children just need to bump up against the consequences of their behavior a few times before they get it and begin making different choices. A few continue to make choices that create negative effects in their lives. Have faith in the process and continue your consistent efforts.

Is it respectful? Yes, if you don't make them wrong,

bad, lazy, inconsiderate, dumb, forgetful, obnoxious, or ridiculous. Just make them someone who has chosen the consequence and someone who gets to experience that outcome. And do it with love in your heart.

Will it help you become the parent you always wanted to be? Only you can answer that because you are the only one who knows what the parent you always wanted to be looks, sounds, and acts like.

What will it teach? Only your children can decide that. They choose what meaning to take from the lessons you offer. They choose what to let in and what to resist. They know better than we do the lessons they most need to learn. Potential lessons abound. Your job is to hold the door open. It is up to them to decide whether or not to walk through.

Chapter Four

PUTTING IT ALL TOGETHER

The Wilson's young son has a habit of interrupting when his mother is on the telephone. He can be play-ing quietly, totally engrossed in whatever is before him, without any thought of needing attention - until the phone rings. That's when the interrupting begins.

"Mommy," he says, as he stands before her. "Mommy," he repeats louder if he gets no response. Ignoring the youngster's pleading doesn't work. Turning a back to this child only serves to increase his resolve to make his presence known. The increasing frequency and volume of "Mommy, Mommy, Mommy" can be heard clearly on the other end of the line. It is distracting to both parties.

What's a parent to do? Should this parent use the One-Minute Behavior Modifier? Clearly, Mrs. Wilson could state, "Lawrence, that is interrupting. In this family, we don't interrupt when someone is on the telephone because it distracts the person who is talking and they aren't able to concentrate. What is needed when you want my attention is to quietly place your hand on my elbow. This will be your signal to me that you want my attention. I will wink at you, which means I noticed the signal and that I will give you some atten-tion when I come to a break in the conversation. Thank you for your cooperation."

Or should Mrs. Wilson use the Dynamic Discipline Equation? If she selected that parenting strategy, her words could have been, "Lawrence, in our family, opportunity equals responsibility. You have the opportunity to stay in the kitchen with me while I'm on the phone. Your responsibility is to let me complete my conversation without interrupting or send me a signal that you want a turn by touching my elbow. If you choose to continue to interrupt, you will be choosing to have a different opportunity when I'm on the phone."

Another scenario might find Mrs. Wilson feeling increasingly annoyed as her son persists in calling, "Mommy," while she is engaged in a conversation on the telephone. When her son's interruptions exceed his mother's tolerance level, she may explode in anger. Hopefully, her anger will be strategically controlled through the use of the Positive Anger Explosion.

"Lawrence," she could say. "I heard several interruptions when I was on the phone. I'm annoyed and frustrated because I wasn't able to concentrate on my conversation with your father. A hand on my elbow is what will get my positive attention when I'm on the phone."

What Comes First?

Which strategy should Mrs. Wilson use first? Where should she begin? What is the correct order when using the only three discipline strategies you will ever need?

When using these invaluable techniques, there is no preferred order. As you can see from *Diagram A* (next page), the three discipline strategies are displayed in a circle.

Diagram A

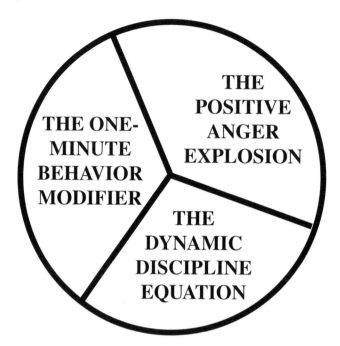

It is no accident that these three influential strategies are not displayed in stepwise fashion. That's because they are not steps that need to be taken in a precise order.

One strategy is no more important than another. Notice that the three discipline strategies are represented by pieces of the circle that are of equal size. If they were removed from the circle, the pieces could be placed back in any order to complete the picture. The three integral pieces of the pie can be arranged in different combinations and still create the perfect circle, as shown in Diagrams B, C, and D.

B.

C.

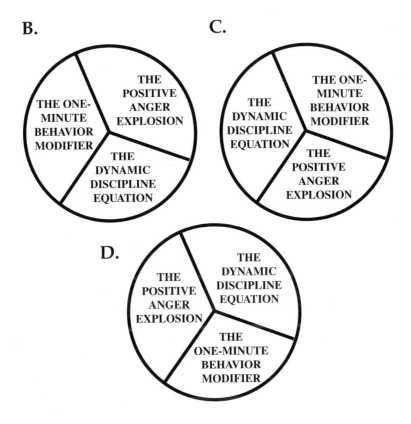

D.

Notice also that all three strategies touch each other. They are connected and when used together create a larger whole that is designed to become the core of your discipline repertoire.

Mrs. Wilson can begin with any one of the three, equally valuable, responses. We suggest she begin whenever she becomes conscious that a parenting move is needed. If she doesn't realize what is happening until she feels extreme irritation, she may begin with the Positive Anger Explosion. If she notices the interruption the first time it occurs, she could immediately use the One-Minute Behavior Modifier. She may choose to use this strategy several times in order to get the results she wants. If she has used the

Positive Anger Explosion and the One-Minute Behavior Modifier with minimal success, it may be time for her to consider using the Dynamic Discipline Equation.

Adding Other Strategies

"I want to use empathy with my child," a father told us at a conference where we presented these three strategies. "You don't mention anything about empathy."

Remember the carpenter in the introduction? He carried three tools with him everywhere he went. They were the three tools he would need to complete most jobs: a hammer, a screwdriver, and a saw.

There will come a time in this carpenter's life when he will want to do a finer job and become more specific with his finishing skills. As he becomes more skilled with the basic tools of his trade, he will want to add more options to his toolbox. At that time he may add a sander, a drill, or a plane. Even then, he will still rely most often on the original three tools.

The same holds for you as a parent. The three discipline strategies presented in this book are the ones you need most, the ones you will most likely use, the ones that will give you the best chance of completing most parenting jobs successfully. Certainly you may add other skills to your toolbox to fine-tune your skills in the sacred role of parenting. You may choose to add empathy, learn to praise nonevaluatively, or develop any of the other skills we present in our previous parenting books, *Parent Talk: How to Talk to Your Children in Language That Builds Self-Esteem and Encourages Responsibility and The 10 Commitments: Parenting with*

Purpose. (See www.personalpowerpress.com for a listing of all of our products.) If you're looking to expand your parenting toolbox, these two books are a wonderful place to begin, as they are filled with practical skills you can put to use immediately to support the basic three that we present here.

Still, no matter how many other parenting skills you fit in your toolbox, these are the three that you will use the most. They are the three you will take with you everywhere you go. They are the ones you will need most whether you're working with your own youngsters or with other people's children.

An expanded diagram of the only three discipline strategies you will ever need is provided below.

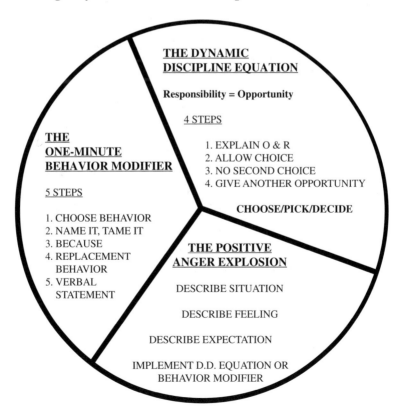

THE DYNAMIC
DISCIPLINE EQUATION

Responsibility = Opportunity

4 STEPS

1. EXPLAIN O & R
2. ALLOW CHOICE
3. NO SECOND CHOICE
4. GIVE ANOTHER OPPORTUNITY

CHOOSE/PICK/DECIDE

THE
ONE-MINUTE
BEHAVIOR MODIFIER

5 STEPS

1. CHOOSE BEHAVIOR
2. NAME IT, TAME IT
3. BECAUSE
4. REPLACEMENT
   BEHAVIOR
5. VERBAL
   STATEMENT

THE POSITIVE
ANGER EXPLOSION

DESCRIBE SITUATION

DESCRIBE FEELING

DESCRIBE EXPECTATION

IMPLEMENT D.D. EQUATION OR
BEHAVIOR MODIFIER

All three of the basic strategies presented here do much more than simply discipline your children.

First, they each teach. The One-Minute Behavior Modifier teaches the new behavior that you want to have replace the undesired one. The Dynamic Discipline Equation teaches the relationship between cause and effect: *if you choose this, you create that.* The Positive Anger Explosion teaches your child the impact his behavior is having on you and describes the expected behavior. It also teaches how to communicate anger cleanly without wounding the spirit and how to communicate respectfully in times of stress.

Second, each of these strategies allows the child to do her own thinking. Telling children what to do, issuing commands, and telling them to stop behaviors trains them to expect others to do their thinking for them. Examine each one carefully and you will see that none of them tells the child what to do. Each one lets the child think for herself and be the creator of the outcomes that flow from her choices.

Third, all three strategies parent from the end first. They help you stay conscious that in this present moment your goal is not so much to eliminate this perturbing situation as it is to raise a responsible, caring, confident child who can leave home someday as a young adult ready to face the world with skills and an attitude that will serve him well his entire life. Each one of these techniques helps the child to become decisionally literate, personally empowered, and able to function as a responsible, capable human being. Each one helps you prepare your child for a successful life.

A final characteristic that these three practical strategies share is that they allow you to become the parent you always wanted to be. Haven't you always wanted to be the teacher rather than the criticizer or shamer? Haven't you always wanted to be the center that holds, even as change, challenge, and sometimes chaos swirls around you? Haven't you wanted the skills necessary to make yourself an inspirational parent who invites appropriate behavior while holding children accountable with an open heart regardless of the outcomes they choose?

Now, with these three dynamic and workable strategies, you can be the parent you always wanted to be. And by changing yourself first, by becoming more skillful with the only three discipline strategies you will ever need, you will lovingly and consistently invite your children to choose respectful, responsible behaviors that match with your family values. In changing yourself first, you will take charge of your family life by controlling your own behavior. You will make yourself increasingly dispensable so that your child can become increasingly self-motivating, self-reliant, and self-responsible.

No one does perfect parenting. No one gets perfect parenting. What all children deserve most is a parent who works at improving his or her attitude and actions in regard to the important responsibility of being a parent. Use this book to refine your skills. Practice. Improve. And continue to grow along with your children.

They're worth it. And so are you!

A B O U T   T H E   A U T H O R S

Portraits by Gregg

Chick Moorman

Chick Moorman is the director of the Institute for Personal Power, a consulting firm dedicated to providing high-quality professional development activities for educators and parents.

He is a former classroom teacher with over forty-five years of experience in the field of education. His mission is to help people experience a greater sense of personal power in their lives so they can in turn empower others.

Chick conducts full-day workshops and seminars for school districts and parent groups. He also delivers keynote addresses for local, state, and national conferences.

He is available for the following topic areas:

FOR EDUCATORS

- *Achievement Motivation and Behavior Management through Effective Teacher Talk*
- *Motivating the Unmotivated*
- *Teaching Respect and Responsibility*
- *Celebrate the Spirit Whisperers*

FOR PARENTS

- *Parent Talk: Words That Empower, Words That Wound*
- *Transformational Parenting*
- *Raising Response-Able Children*
- *The Only Three Parenting Strategies You'll Ever Need*
- *Parenting with Purpose*

If you would like more information about these programs or would like to discuss a possible training or speaking date, please contact:

Chick Moorman
P.O. Box 547
Merrill, MI 48637
Telephone: (877) 360-1477
Fax: (989) 643-5156
E-mail: ipp57@aol.com
Website: www.chickmoorman.com

Portraits by Gregg

Thomas B. Haller,
MDiv, LMSW, ACSW, DST

Thomas Haller is the founder and director of Healing Minds Institute, a center devoted to empowering individuals with skills for creating interpersonal change, building relationship success, and raising responsible children.

He has maintained a private practice for over eighteen years in Bay City, Michigan, as a child, adolescent and couples therapist and an AASECT certified diplomate of sex therapy. Thomas is known locally as "The Love Doctor," appearing on a weekly morning radio program answering relationship and parenting questions on air.

As a widely sought-after national and international presenter, Thomas conducts full-day workshops and seminars for churches, school districts, parent groups, and counseling agencies.

He is also a regular lecturer at universities across the country.

Thomas is available for the following topic areas:

FOR COUPLES

- *The 7 Keys to Creating a Successful Relationship*
- *How to Talk to Your Partner about Sex*
- *The Language of Mutual Respect and Intimacy*
- *The 20 Best and 20 Worst Things to Say to Your Partner*
- *Success 101: How to Be Successful at Whatever You Do*

FOR PARENTS

- *The 10 Commitments to Parenting with Purpose*
- *The Only Three Parenting Strategies You'll Ever Need*
- *How to Talk to Your Children about Sex*
- *How to Inspire Children to Write*
- *Managing Aggression and Anger in Children*

Want a customized workshop? Thomas will structure a workshop to meet your needs.

For more information about these programs or to discuss a possible training or speaking date, please contact:

Thomas Haller: Haller's Healing Minds, Inc.
5225 Three Mile Rd.
Bay City, MI 48706
Telephone: (989) 686-5356
Fax: (989) 643-5156
E-mail: thomas@thomashaller.com
Website: www.thomashaller.com

OTHER BOOKS AND PRODUCTS

www.personalpowerpress.com

For Parents

THE 10 COMMITMENTS: *Parenting with Purpose,* by Chick Moorman and Thomas Haller ($20.00)

PARENT TALK: *How to Talk to Your Children in Language That Builds Self-Esteem and Encourages Responsibility,* by Chick Moorman ($14.00)

THE PARENT ADVISOR: *60 Articles to Ease Your Parenting Concerns,* CD by Chick Moorman and Thomas Haller ($19.95)

THE LANGUAGE OF RESPONSE-ABLE PARENTING, 5-CD set featuring Chick Moorman ($39.50)

THE PARENT TALK SYSTEM: *The Language of Response-Able Parenting, Facilitator's Manual*, by Chick Moorman, Sarah Knapp, and Judith Minton ($300.00)

PARENT TALK FOCUS CARDS, by Chick Moorman ($10.00)

WINNING THE WHINING WARS, DVD by Thomas Haller ($19.95)

INSPIRING CHILDREN TO WRITE, DVD by Thomas Haller and Reese Haller ($19.95)

WHERE THE HEART IS: *Stories of Home and Family*, by Chick Moorman ($15.00)

For Educators

SPIRIT WHISPERERS: *Teachers Who Nourish a Child's Spirit*, by Chick Moorman ($25.00)

TEACHER TALK: *What It Really Means*, by Chick Moorman and Nancy Weber ($15.00)

OUR CLASSROOM: *We Can Learn Together*, by Chick Moorman and Dee Dishon ($20.00)

Miscellaneous

COUPLE TALK: *How to Talk Your Way to a Great Relationship*, by Chick Moorman and Thomas Haller ($25.00)

DENTAL TALK: *How to Manage Children's Behavior with Effective Verbal Skills*, by Thomas Haller and Chick Moorman ($25.00)

TALK SENSE TO YOURSELF: *The Language of Personal Power*, by Chick Moorman ($15.00)

www.personalpowerpress.com
(877) 360-1477
P.O Box 547
Merrill, MI 48637

<u>OUR VISION:</u>
HEALING ACRES

A portion of the proceeds from all of our books is used to maintain an equine retirement ranch. One dollar from each book sold will go toward the support of **Healing Acres Equine Retirement Ranch.**

The goal of Healing Acres Retirement Ranch is to provide a peaceful and caring environment for aged horses that have devoted many years of service. It will include a low-stress atmosphere, room to exercise and graze freely, adequate shelter, and preventive and attentive health care for all horses.

Other services planned for Healing Acres Retirement Ranch include therapeutic riding for persons with dis-abilities and equine-assisted psychotherapy.

If you wish to make a donation beyond the purchase of this book, please contact Thomas or Chick at the Healing Minds Institute via email at: **thomas@thomashaller.com**

Thank you for helping us support this important vision.